PRAISE FO..

# HOW TO PAY FOR COLLEGE

"No conversation is more fraught with panic and worry than how to pay for college... Ann has solved that problem with this book!"

—Carl Richards, bestselling author, *The Behavior Gap*

"Ann is the expert in everything financial, especially as it relates to college planning. A must read for students, parents, school counselors and all who seek a better understanding of paying for college, budgeting and spending plans."

—Lewis J. DeLuca Jr., director of student financial literacy and advising, Southern Connecticut State University

"*How to Pay For College* is a comprehensive resource that will help any parent or financial advisor navigate the complex process of funding higher education costs. The book covers everything from how to fill out the FAFSA (financial aid application) to how to find scholarships and what types of loans are available. Ann Garcia breaks the process down systematically and provides insights that help reduce the sense of overwhelm. She says that you don't have to plan for all of those possibilities. You only need to plan for the ones that work for your family. As a parent of two college students, her own experiences and commentary certainly make me feel more confident in managing this process. I will be using *HTPFC* in my work with clients who are facing this situation in their lives, as well as personally, as I am preparing to enter this phase with my oldest daughter."

—Danika Waddell, CFP®, RLP®, CSLP®, president and founder, Xena Financial Planning

"Ann Garcia (aka The College Financial Lady) has expertly guided students and their families through the process of college admissions and financial planning. She also went through the process herself recently as the mother of twins. Ann generously makes a wealth of information freely available through her posts on social media, email newsletter, website, and podcast. All of these resources are fabulous, so it is no surprise that this book is no different! It has already become a staple in my work as a public high school counselor! Though my two children are young, it is an invaluable resource as my wife and I plan for their college education. Anyone who works with college-bound students or has one in their life should make this book part of their collection!"

—John McMichael, assistant principal for student personnel services, Audubon Jr–Sr High School


"Families have many more college choices than they think, but the complexity of our system makes it hard to find them. Ann's book walks parents through the steps of developing a college plan—from researching colleges to filing the FAFSA to talking about money— which opens up a range of choices that fit the student's academic and personal profile and the family's budget."

—Terry Mady-Grove, JD, MA, CEP, president and founder, Charted University Consultants, LLC

"As a CERTIFIED FINANCIAL PLANNER™ professional and parent, I use the powerful wisdom that Ann shares in this book to guide both my client conversations as well as decisions my spouse and I make for our kids."

—Andy Mardock, MBA, CFP®, founder and president, ViviFi Planning

# HOW TO
# PAY FOR
# COLLEGE

Every owner of a physical copy of this edition of

# HOW TO PAY FOR COLLEGE

can download the eBook for free direct from us at Harriman House, in a DRM-free format that can be read on any eReader, tablet or smartphone.

Simply head to:

**ebooks.harriman-house.com/howtopayforcollege**

to get your copy now.

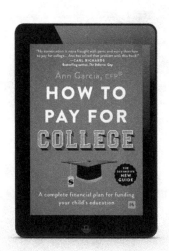

# HOW TO
# PAY FOR
# COLLEGE

A complete financial
plan for funding your
child's education

## ANN GARCIA

HARRIMAN HOUSE LTD
3 Viceroy Court
Bedford Road
Petersfield
Hampshire
GU32 3LJ
GREAT BRITAIN
Tel: +44 (0)1730 233870

Email: enquiries@harriman-house.com
Website: harriman.house

First published in 2022.
Copyright © Ann Garcia

Paperback ISBN: 978-0-85719-929-4
eBook ISBN: 978-0-85719-930-0

British Library Cataloguing in Publication Data
A CIP catalogue record for this book can be obtained from the British Library.

# CONTENTS

# INTRODUCTION

**W**HEN I TELL people where my twins go to college, the typical reaction is, "Wow, that sounds expensive!" And yes, it does sound expensive. My daughter Gabi attends the world's most expensive university, the University of Chicago; her brother Alex goes to the University of Arizona. Since we live in Oregon, that's an out-of-state public school for us.

It may surprise you to learn that neither college costs much more than our in-state flagship public school. Fortunately, both colleges are extremely generous with financial aid and scholarships, making it possible for both of my kids to attend their top choice school. Beyond the money, I'm grateful for the opportunities these choices created for my kids to experience life in different parts of the country and get outside their comfort zones by attending colleges where they didn't know anyone.

Here's the thing: We didn't just get lucky and get great scholarship offers. We did our homework to find colleges that fit each of them socially and academically, and that were likely to offer them scholarship packages that would make acceptance possible. And that's what I want to help you do too.

As a financial advisor, I spend my days helping people meet their financial goals and make good decisions about how they save and spend their money. For a long time, we advisors have focused on retirement planning because, as the saying goes, "You can take out a loan for college, but not for retirement."

However, I've held meeting after meeting with young adults struggling to plan for anything—buying a home, starting a family, funding a Roth IRA—because they were drowning in student loan debt. I've also met with countless parents who felt that putting their kids through college was going to leave them unable to retire before they turned 90. Both dilemmas led me to realize that good planning for a family's second most expensive goal—educating their children—is an essential component of ensuring their long-term financial security.

Planning for college is the ultimate balancing act of parenting. On the one hand, we want to offer the world of possibility to our kids: As an acknowledgment of their hard work, accomplishments, and their general awesomeness (they're our kids, after all!), and because we want the best possible future for them. On the other hand, the reality of college is that it's just too expensive for most families to make every option available. If we had three hands, the third would be the fear many parents feel: That constraining their child's college choices on the basis of money is akin to visiting the sins of the parent on the child—my inability to give you every option will limit your future.

You're normal if the thought of planning for college stresses you out!

I've spent the better part of the last decade counseling families on college funding and selection strategies. I realized in my client meetings that I was repeating the same things pretty regularly, so I started writing them down in a blog, which expanded my reach to hundreds of thousands more families. I really enjoy seeing the sense of empowerment families get from developing a strategy to get their kids great educations that don't knock their other financial goals out of reach. I'm happy to say I've helped thousands of families save millions of dollars on college—and to welcome you to that group!

Several years into writing the blog, the opportunity to test my system through my own kids' college application process came up. Good news: It worked! Both of my kids found great college fits that also suited our family's finances. We won't have to delay our retirement due to college costs; in fact, we've continued contributing to retirement savings throughout our kids' college years.

This book will walk you step-by-step through the process of preparing for college. You'll learn about savings strategies, how to research colleges to find financial fits, how to find scholarships, and how to develop a spending plan that maximizes free money. I've also got some tips for talking with your kids about money and college costs—because they're on this journey with you. And each chapter includes a worksheet that helps you clarify your thoughts and solidify your plans.

You're right to want your kids to have great college opportunities. I'll help you figure out how to get them!

## How to use this book

My goal in this book is to meet you where you are and walk you down the path to where you need to be. That means that if you haven't started saving for college yet, I'm not going to make you feel guilty. Just follow the instructions for choosing a savings method and do it. If you're a parent of a high school student and just thinking about college for the first time, that's fine too. But please read the information for younger families anyway, because you'll be better off if you take the time to catch up on those tasks.

You might think of this book like a college class. Each chapter contains both written material and a worksheet. The written part is like the lecture, and you'll learn a lot from it. The worksheet is akin to the homework, where you synthesize your new knowledge by applying it to your own situation. Completing the worksheets should give you a pretty detailed plan by the end of the book, so please make them an integral part of your reading. And if you don't like the small print on the worksheets or doing math in your head, or if you're a few years out from college and likely to be revising some of the information over the coming years, you can download them from my website at howtopayforcollege.com/htpfc-book-worksheets

This book is organized sequentially, starting with framing your thinking about college at different ages, then giving you an overview of the college funding landscape, then moving into your own college search and selection process. But you can attack it at your own pace or according to your own priorities; unlike *Game of Thrones*, which I couldn't follow once my husband got a few episodes ahead of me, each chapter here can stand on its own and be read in the order that works for you.

With apologies to those who hate acronyms, college planning is full of jargon, and there's only so many times you can write out Student Aid Index or Qualified Higher Education Expenses. You can always flip to the glossary at the back, which I encourage you to bookmark. Likewise, with apologies to all the young adults in the later stages of high school or early college years, I often refer to the college-bound folks as "kids." This is not meant to be demeaning; it's what I call my own young adult offspring. I try to intersperse "student" in there too, but as you read this book, you'll probably notice that these conversations are at least as much about parenting as they are about finances. Let's face it, though they're not kids, they'll always be *your* kids.

This book might be the only tool you'll need in your college planning process, but you'll also find some suggestions for enlisting other good resources. My hope is that by consolidating this advice that's worked for thousands of families, I can help you put your kid through a college that they'll enjoy and benefit from, and keep the rest of your financial goals within reach, too. Ready to get started? Turn the page, and let's do this!

# CHAPTER 1

# Why College?

## WHAT YOU'LL LEARN IN THIS CHAPTER

Economic and non-economic benefits of college, who gains from attending college and who doesn't, and whether which school you attend matters.

M Y HUSBAND BOB and I are raving fans of our respective alma maters, the University of Michigan and UC Berkeley.

Saturdays find us dressed in blue and gold (he would say maize and blue) yelling at our TV or in the oddball Portland bars that host Michigan or Berkeley football games. Trips home to our families always include a stop on campus to revisit old haunts and relive memories.

Each of us firmly believes that the specific experiences we had at our respective colleges are foundational pieces of who we are, far beyond just our careers. We're active in our alumni associations and, despite the years and the miles, count college friends among our nearest and dearest.

Our kids, twins Alex and Gabi, own Michigan and Cal gear in every size up to 10. Why up to 10? Because right around that point we realized that as much as we love our schools, there was no chance that we would send our kids to either of them. Michigan and Berkeley rank at or near the top on countless metrics, but not one of our most important ones: Generosity to out-of-state students. That meant that neither school was likely to meet the budget constraints we put on our children's college searches.

Let's be honest: Our generation had a different set of college choices than our kids do. Tuition inflation has outpaced normal inflation such that private colleges often have list prices in excess of the median family income of about $69,000; many in-state public colleges cost one-third of the median family income. That means we can't frame our kids' college choices through the lens of our choices, and instead we need to focus on college goals: Career opportunities, independence, personal growth, learning, and all the incredible experiences that are part of the college years.

For my family, it also meant we needed to reframe our conversations with our kids about college away from Michigan and Berkeley toward college in general, or from "which college" to "why college." Because which college you go to doesn't have nearly the lifelong impact of whether or not you go to college... and how you pay for it.

## The benefits of a college degree

It's probably no surprise that college graduates enjoy lower unemployment rates and higher incomes than do those without college education. But the benefits of a degree extend well beyond economic outcomes. Those with college degrees consistently score higher in life satisfaction and happiness surveys. They are more likely to marry and less likely to divorce. College graduates even live longer and healthier lives.[1]

So there are great reasons to want your kids to attend college, beyond the life experience or attempts to keep up with the Joneses. Despite rising costs, a college degree remains a good investment, with both qualitative and quantitative returns. You're right to want this for your children.

In 2015 the Social Security Administration estimated the present value of a college degree, based on increased lifetime earnings, as $260,000 for men and $180,000 for women.[2] This was based on college-educated men earning $900,000 more over their lifetimes than those with only a high school diploma. For women, the difference was $655,000. Men with graduate degrees earned $1.5 million more; women, $1.1 million more.

That doesn't mean that it makes sense for a woman to borrow $180,000 to finance college, because borrowing that much would lead to loan payments stripping out the incremental value of the degree. But it does mean that college is likely to be a good investment, and a reasonable amount of borrowing is acceptable if it makes college attendance and graduation possible.

Crises really hammer home the importance of a college degree in the workforce: When Great Recession unemployment peaked in February 2010, the unemployment rate was 11% for high school graduates with no college, but less than half of that (under 5%) for those with a bachelor's degree. In April 2020—the height of pandemic-related unemployment—the unemployment rate was over 17% for high school graduates, compared with 8% for those holding a bachelor's degree.[3]

All of that seems really obvious. But did you know that the more education you have, the less likely you are to die of heart disease or to have Type 2 diabetes? There's an income component to those data points, too, which also skews heavily in favor of college: Median earnings for those with a bachelor's degree are about 65% higher than for those with only a high school diploma. This earnings gap starts early: Among 25–34-year-olds, median incomes for college graduates were 57% higher than those of high school graduates.

Earnings also keep up with reasonable student loan debt. In this book, "reasonable student loan debt" is the federal Direct Student Loan. Students can borrow $27,000 over four years in the federal loan programs; those who do so will pay approximately $325 per month for 10 years to pay off their debt. Median income for a young college graduate is about $1,650 higher each month than the median for those with only a high school diploma, meaning you're better off taking on some debt to earn a college degree than skipping college to avoid borrowing.

## Who doesn't benefit from college?

There's one group who not only doesn't benefit from college but who ends up worse off for having gone: Those who enroll, take out student loans, and don't finish college. And of course, when I talk about "college" in this book, I'm talking about public and private nonprofit bachelors degree-granting institutions and the pathways such as community college that might get a person there. Because there's a second group of college students who are generally worse for wear after attending college: Those who attend for-profit institutions, where the degree is often not worth the paper it's printed on. When you think of for-profit colleges, think of the semi-predatory schools that periodically appear in news headlines for defrauding students, charging tuition that has no relation to potential earnings, and otherwise taking advantage of young people who have been told that education is the key to their future.

## *Why* college, not *which* college

Did you notice something in those statistics? The phrase I used was "college graduates" and not "graduates of ___ college." That's because there's a large and growing body of research showing that good outcomes do not depend on *which* college you attend. This is an important consideration for families who might be presented with college options with price tags ranging anywhere from $12,000 to $82,000 annually, as was my family.

This is something you may need to reassure yourself (as well as your kid) of throughout the process: Spending more on college does not guarantee a better outcome; spending less doesn't risk a worse outcome. (Feel free to chant this like a mantra.)

What creates bad college outcomes? Not graduating. Graduating with too much debt. Picking the wrong school, transferring and ending up on the six-year plan with only enough money for four years, thus graduating with too much debt.

You probably get the picture, but since this chapter is chock-full of statistics, here are a few more:

- The national homeownership rate among young adults decreased by 2% from 2005 to 2014, a decline which is largely attributed to student loan debt.[4]

- Higher student loan debt correlates with lower marriage rates and parenthood: Research shows that every $10,000 in student loan debt decreases the likelihood of marriage by 3–4%.[5]

- Student loan debt decreases graduate school enrollment and pursuit of public-sector employment.

- Young adults with student loan debt are more likely to live with their parents. Not only might that drive you all nuts, but it also limits employment opportunities to those in your hometown— which might not be New York, Seattle or San Jose.

Another mantra, therefore, that you should be asking is "why college?" and not "which college?"

"Why college" creates choices. Lots and lots of colleges and universities, at all different price points, can give you the career opportunities, independence, personal growth, learning and incredible experiences that are part of the college years. Whereas focusing on "which college" creates pressure and artificial constraints that aren't backed up by data. Consider:

- The alma mater of the most Fortune 500 CEOs? Texas A&M. Penn State counts more Fortune 500 CEOs than either Stanford or Harvard.

- Harvard rejected Warren Buffett, John Kerry, Tom Brokaw, and Ted Turner, but accepted Ted Kaczynski.

- According to the National Bureau of Economic Research, "Students who attended more selective colleges do not earn more than other students who were accepted and rejected by comparable schools but attended less selective colleges." (The exception is that attending elite colleges does provide greater advantages to students from more disadvantaged family backgrounds.)[6]

- Among 2020's Rhodes Scholarship recipients, a quarter attended public universities that accept more than 50% of applicants. Among the schools that have produced Rhodes Scholars in the 2010s are UMBC, University of Oklahoma, Southern Connecticut State University, UC Santa Cruz, South Dakota State University, the Air Force Academy, and the Naval Academy.

My point is not to denigrate any school, but rather to show you that many, many colleges and universities prepare students to succeed at the highest levels. By being open to a variety of college choices, you open the door to a college plan that meets your family's budget and gets your student an excellent education with a minimum of debt for either of you.

Just as my husband and I stopped going all-in on our schools' gear, I want you to shift your thinking from wanting your child to attend a specific college to why you want your student to go to college in the first place. Such as:

- Increasing their knowledge and understanding of the world.

- Preparing for a broader range of career paths.

- Improving their critical thinking skills.

- Getting exposure to new ideas and a different set of people.

- Living healthier, happier lives.

Then think of the experiences you want them to have in college, such as:

- Study abroad.

- Greek life.

- Internships and research opportunities.

- Pursuing a passion alongside a pre-professional curriculum. For my daughter, that's a double major in computer science and classics with a part-time job at the on-campus theater.

So as much as you (or your kid) may think the top priority is a specific college's name on the top of their diploma in a few years, in actuality, you both want the *outcomes* college provides, which are offered by a wide range of colleges. In addition, you probably want your kids to be able to participate in the fun and enriching things you consider part of the overall college experience. Together, we can make it happen.

Ready to get started? Turn the page for a worksheet on your college values.

# WORKSHEET 1: YOUR COLLEGE VALUES AND PRIORITIES

To download this worksheet, go to howtopayforcollege.com/htpfc-book-worksheets.

❑ Please list either three favorite memories from your own college education, or three things you most wished you had a chance to experience in college.

_____

❑ What experiences do you most want your children to have during their college years?

_____

❑ How has your college education or lack of a college education shaped your life?

_____

❑ Did you borrow to attend college? If so, how long did it take you to pay off your student loans? How did student loan debt impact your choices or lifestyle as a young adult? If you knew then what you know now, would you choose the same path?

_____

❑ Why did you choose the college you chose? Would you choose it again?

_____

# CHAPTER 2

# What Does College Cost?

## WHAT YOU'LL LEARN IN THIS CHAPTER

Why college costs so much, how to avoid the traps that can make college more expensive, determining the net cost vs the list price, and what "free college" means.

M Y DAUGHTER GABI applied to eight colleges and was accepted to six. Her awards from these schools resulted in net prices ranging from about $12,000 to $57,000 per year. This was after we had pared down her application list by eliminating any whose net price calculators and other available scholarships showed that her cost of attendance was unlikely to meet our family's budget. This mind-boggling range of prices is probably familiar to anyone with a child who has gone through the college application process.

Actual college costs—at least for private schools—are extraordinarily opaque. While published list prices may range north of $80,000, colleges employ a variety of tools to reduce costs for desirable students, such that the average tuition discount rate—the percent of list cost that is not actually paid—reached 53.9% for the 2020–2021 school year. That means that for every $100 of tuition charged, only $46.10 is actually collected. The rest is eliminated through scholarships and grants.

Yet averages don't tell the full story. After all, the average American family has 1.93 children, but you don't ever see .93 of a child walking around. Similarly, you should not expect that every college will discount your tuition by 54%.

One of the most common questions families ask is, "How can I plan for college if I don't know where my child is going to go?" After all, planning for a range of outcomes that could vary by $200,000 or more per child is the ultimate moving-goalposts challenge.

Here's the secret: You don't have to plan for all of those possibilities. You only need to plan for the ones that work for your family. Because if you're willing to use the "why college?" approach instead of the "which college?" approach, your student can tailor their search to schools that are likely to be affordable to you.

Picture a different family milestone: After a decade of road trips, carpools, and toting the family around town, it's time to trade in the trusty minivan. You head to the car dealership, where you're offered $5,000 for the trade-in, and off you go to pick your new ride. You see a splash of yellow over in a corner of the lot. "Yellow is my favorite color!" you tell yourself, and you head over. Seeing that it's a Ferrari Tributo, you ignore the $280,000 price tag—that's what car loans are for—and hop in…

Actually, you don't—because that would be absurd. It's probably more likely that you research what you'll get for your used car, decide how much you can afford to spend on a new car, and then start looking for cars with the features you like in that price range.

Just as you shop for cars or a house based on what you can afford, so should you shop for college. The "cost of college" that you're going to plan for is the cost of colleges within a range that your family can afford. And as is the case with cars, you'll find a wide variety of choices in your target price range.

# Why college costs so much now

## The free market

As you probably already know, the cost of college has soared over recent decades, far outpacing inflation or growth in household incomes. Most public universities did not charge tuition through the 1960s; during that decade, Baby Boomers' demand for higher education began to outpace supply, and public universities began charging nominal tuition. In 1980 the average annual tuition at public four-year colleges was $804; by 1990 it had only gone up to $1,888. By 2020, it was $16,647. To me, one of the most astonishing aspects of the pushback against free college proposals is that it seems to be coming mostly from the generation for whom public colleges were free or virtually free.

Cost of attendance at public universities increased by almost 500% in the 30 years from 1986 to 2016. Private college costs increased by a mere 467% in that time period. Meanwhile, median household income increased by a whopping 14%. In fact, in the 1985–86 school year, average public college costs were just under 14% of median family income; private colleges cost 33% of median family income. In 2015–16, those numbers were 27% and 56%. How is it possible that colleges charge prices that are unaffordable to families?

The simple answer is *because they can*.

It's important to remember that colleges are businesses, and businesses set prices based on supply and demand. A college prices its services more like an airline than a grocery store. On any given flight, passengers are paying a variety of prices for essentially the same thing, and colleges operate similarly. Just looking at the demand side, at selective private colleges typically one-quarter to one-third of applicants don't even file a FAFSA or CSS Profile. That means that between one-quarter to one-third of students are expecting to pay the full sticker price.

Why would a college *not* accept full price from them? On the other hand, that leaves the college with somewhere between two-thirds and three-quarters of its student body remaining to be filled, and by a population that can't or won't pay full price. So just like an airline trying to fill every seat on a plane, colleges discount tuition and offer other incentives to prospective students to get them to enroll.

In addition to the free market argument, there are plenty more complex reasons why college costs so much more today than it did a generation ago.

## Declining state funding and increasing state costs

Higher education tends to be one of the most vulnerable items in a state's budget, if for no other reason than that it's one of the few items that has an alternative funding means—namely passing along the costs to the consumer. Starting in the 1970s, initiatives limiting property tax increases began taking hold across the country. With about 18% of state budgets going to higher education, reductions in tax revenue impact higher education funding. In addition, pension and healthcare costs have soared in the past several decades, meaning that an increasing share of funds going to public higher education is going to benefits for employees, not students. Finally, few states have returned to pre-Great Recession-level spending on higher education, and the pandemic has wreaked further havoc on many states' budgets (fortunately, other than a few that are highly impacted by lost tourism revenue, most states have at least held higher education funding steady through the pandemic).

## Increased administrative and services costs

Salaries for college presidents have increased dramatically over the past several decades. In 2019, 81 college presidents earned over $1 million annually. Other administrative areas, including fundraising and financial aid have ballooned as well. Spending on student services, including counseling, tutoring, gyms, and improvements to dorms, has also increased.

## Increased availability of financial aid, especially loans

A number of studies have shown that when more financial aid becomes available, schools respond by raising prices. A 2017 study by the New York Fed, for example, determined that a $1 increase in the subsidized Direct Student Loan amount resulted in a 60 cent increase in tuition, with smaller increases resulting from changes to unsubsidized loans. Another study found that decreasing availability of Parent PLUS loans resulted in tuition deflation.[1]

## More students going to college

Many studies have pointed out that state funding for higher education has remained more or less constant, adjusted for inflation. How is it, then, that funding for students has decreased? Because more students are attending college. In 1990, public colleges and universities enrolled 9.7 million students. By 2020, that number had increased by a third, to 13.1 million.[2] So even if funding levels kept pace with inflation, they didn't keep pace with increasing enrollment—which, in addition to requiring additional per-student funding, often resulted in the need to invest further in campus facilities to accommodate larger enrollments.

As you can see, there are a lot of supply-side reasons why college costs so much. But there are plenty of other factors within your control that can add to the cost of college.

## The traps that lead to creeping college costs

There are plenty of institutional and external forces driving up the cost of college, but students and families also play a role. One important reason college can be more expensive than you planned is students taking longer than four years to graduate. Often this results from transferring, in particular because the new school may or may not give full credit for coursework at the original school. Sometimes students transfer for their own reasons—discovering that the school they loved on paper isn't as great in reality, or choosing a major or career path that their school doesn't offer, or starting at a community college before transferring and finishing at a four-year college, for example. In other cases, schools close down and students are forced to find a new college. Whatever the case, adding an extra year to your studies increases your cost by at least 25%.

Transferring can be expensive even if the student still graduates on time. That's because most schools are far less generous with scholarships for transfer students than with incoming freshmen, so students often end up paying more at the new school due to ineligibility for scholarships.

For example, as of this writing, the highest merit award for incoming freshmen at the University of Oregon is $15,000 annually (a student receiving the Summit and Presidential award), and those scholarships renew automatically for four years. Transfer students, on the other hand, are eligible for a maximum of $3,000 in merit aid and must reapply every year.

Similarly, the University of Florida offers up to $10,000 in merit aid to freshmen; the Office of Admissions offers *no* scholarship opportunities for transfer students. (There are two scholarships offered by the Office of Undergraduate Affairs dedicated to Florida College Transfers for a maximum of $4,000 and offered to a total of 12 students, with only two receiving the maximum $4,000 award.)

Then there are specific costs associated with a particular school your student might choose or the path they follow. Will they participate in study abroad? Are they pursuing a major with a lot of lab classes or that has extra fees?

At some schools, most of the social life—not just parties and events, but intramural sports and other activities—revolves around the Greek system.

Out-of-state schools require travel home for holidays or parent visits. Colleges in high cost of living areas tend to have higher room and board costs.

Some colleges only offer unlimited meal plans.

Some majors require a lot of textbooks.

At some colleges, a student might need a car in order to get a job.

I'm not trying to frighten you, just to help you get a sense of all the components of college cost.

## The deal with "free college"

With all the talk in the news about free college, why are we even talking about what college costs?

Probably because a better way of thinking about free college is the idea that expenses for your lowest-cost choice might be slightly lower in the future than they are today. Most free college proposals fall roughly along the lines of the College For All Act, introduced by Senator Bernie Sanders and Representative Pramila Jayapal. The College for All Act includes:

- Tuition-free community college for all students.

- Tuition-free public colleges and universities and Historically Black Colleges and Universities (HBCUs) for students from families earning less than $125,000.

- Doubling the maximum Pell Grant to $12,990 and allowing its use for non-tuition expenses including room and board, and books.

First and foremost, these changes would be a tremendous benefit to about 75% of U.S. households who would qualify for free tuition based on the income limit. But there are some caveats:

Free college does not mean "everyone goes where they want for free." Notably absent from the list of eligible institutions are private colleges, which currently educate more than a quarter of college students.

"Free" refers to tuition only. Most students would still be on the hook for room and board, and books.

## The bottom line

College only costs what you are willing to pay. Your job as a parent is to help your student figure out what's important for them to succeed in college and to identify schools that provide that at a cost that works for your family.

What we're going to do over the course of this book is map out a plan for your family to get your kids through college without wrecking your retirement or their future. Your kids are going to have a lot of good choices.

Turn the page for a worksheet to get you started.

## WORKSHEET 2: YOUR STUDENT—PAST, PRESENT AND FUTURE

To download this worksheet, go to howtopayforcollege.com/htpfc-book-worksheets.

❏ Picture your student at 25. What does their life look like? Are they engaged in a career? In graduate school? Pursuing a passion? Be as specific as you like.

_____

❏ Picture your student at 30. What does their life look like?

_____

❏ What aspects of school make your student feel the most successful? For example, in-class discussions, homework, test taking.

_____

❏ What aspects of school make your student feel the least successful?

_____

❏ Does your student interact easily with teachers, coaches and other adults in their life?

_____

❏ Thinking of your student's personality and interests, what types of career paths do you envision them pursuing?

_____

❑   Think of an instance when your student had a big win outside of school. What were the drivers of that win? What motivated them to succeed? How did they overcome obstacles along the way?

_____

❑   When is your student happiest?

_____

❑   Why has your student chosen the activities that they participate in? Because friends participate? A particular skill or talent that they've honed over the years? Personal interest?

_____

❑   Is your student comfortable participating in activities with or without their friends?

_____

❑   How does your student meet people and make friends?

_____

❑   What colleges does your student (or, depending on their age, you) think are interesting?

_____

❑   What feels to you like a reasonable amount to spend on college, per student?

_____

# CHAPTER 3

# Developing a College Plan

## WHAT YOU'LL LEARN IN THIS CHAPTER

Age-appropriate college planning steps from newborn through high school, conversation prompts for discussing college with your child.

M Y SON ALEX applied to two schools: University of Oregon (which is in-state for us) and University of Arizona, where he was eligible for a sizable scholarship due to his test scores. Even with the scholarship, Arizona looked like it would cost at least $7,000 more annually than Oregon. Since he had everything ready in time for the deadline, he submitted Early Action (nonbinding) applications to both, submitting online on October 31. And here the paths diverged.

On November 2, as in only *two days later*, he got an acceptance letter from Arizona along with a huge congratulations letter for the substantial scholarship ($18,000 annually) he was awarded. On November 4, he got a big packet in the mail confirming his acceptance and scholarship, along with some logo stickers ("Put one on your phone! Put one on your laptop!").

The following week he was invited to a campus open house in late January. (Did I mention we live in Portland, Oregon and University of Arizona is in Tucson... a far sunnier, warmer place in January?) I got emails from the campus store linking to sweatshirts I could buy him to celebrate his acceptance. He received emails about on-campus housing, reminding him that as soon as he accepted, he would get his housing preference number—and look, this dorm has a pool!

In short, Arizona wanted him to accept, was making him feel very special, and was informing him of all the great things about their school. All the while, we watched his interest in Arizona grow and got this gnawing feeling thinking about the 28,000 extra dollars it would cost over the in-state option.

What about Oregon? They sent an email confirming they had received his application, and then... crickets. After several weeks, during which time a number of his friends had received admissions offers from Oregon, I logged onto his portal with him to confirm that his application was complete, including supporting documentation like transcripts and test scores. Yes, all there. And still no word. Then again, they said they'd respond by December 15, and it was only Thanksgiving week. On December 12, he once again went to his Oregon account to confirm—again—that his application was complete, as he had done on a nearly daily basis for the past two weeks. There, he saw his status had changed from "Processed" to "Admission Offered." But still no email confirmation. And that big acceptance package that his friends keep posting on Snapchat and Instagram? No sign of that, either.

I bring this up because the college application process is not linear, and not all schools respond equally to all students. Some will market to your student aggressively. Others won't. Some will accept them immediately. Others respond on the last possible date. And 17-year-olds don't understand that this is a function of business processes, not love.

That's why it's really important to have a financial plan for college and to talk about money with your student before they get into the application process, well before they set their heart on a school your family can't afford. We were fortunate that, despite all the excitement and hype, Alex understood what it would mean to attend a school that costs an extra $28,000. (Big asterisk here: Please don't think I'm polishing my mom halo about my 17-year-old son's extraordinarily mature approach to this. There was a lot to this conversation which I'll go into in more detail in Chapter 13.)

Unfortunately for many parents, talking with their kids about money is at least as uncomfortable as talking with them about sex. Also unfortunate: Bad financial decisions around college can have similarly deleterious impacts on their future as teenage pregnancy. Parents have told me that talking about money when talking about college feels "dirty," or that putting financial constraints on college decisions feels like punishing your child for your own shortcomings. (Remember your mantra from Chapter 1: Spending more on college does not guarantee a better outcome; spending less doesn't risk a worse outcome.)

When it comes to college, no outside entity will prevent you from making a terrible financial decision. You wouldn't qualify for a mortgage for a house you couldn't afford, but you will be offered student loans for colleges your family can't afford. And just as I don't help my clients with limited means buy villas in Italy for their retirement, I don't recommend that families with limited college savings and cash flow constraints send their children to $75,000-per-year colleges.

And that gets to another piece of this process: What do we want the four-year experience to include? I wanted Alex to be able to study abroad, not have a job his first term in college so he could focus on school, join a fraternity if that's what he wanted, go to sporting events, and participate in intramurals. All of which seemed accessible if he stayed in-state, less so if not.

So before the hype machine cranks up, let's make a plan that works for your family, because plenty of schools have aggressive marketing campaigns that play on the very emotions that are most raw for kids at this point in the process—their need for acceptance, their desire to have their achievements validated, and their quest for an Instagram-worthy acceptance picture.

## Developing your plan

No one should be surprised to find an 18-year-old high school student in their house who is intending to enroll in college. Yet while you've had 18 years to realize this point is coming, every family prioritizes college planning differently, and has different resources available to fund it. And that's fine! As long as your plan isn't just to stick your head in the sand and pretend you don't need to think about this, you'll be OK. The fact that you're even reading this book means that funding college is on your list of priorities and you're taking action to support that. We've got this, no matter what phase of the process you're in.

This chapter includes a timeline for approaching college. Since managing the college selection process is personal finance at its finest—both very personal and very financial—I've included both financial and non-financial steps.

A few ground rules before we get started:

- The purpose of this section is to meet you where you are, not to make you feel guilty for what you haven't done. Just about anything on this list can be done at any point in your journey. If your student is in middle school and this is the first time you've thought about how you'll pay for college, we've got you covered. Just skim the earlier ages to get a few pointers for things you can still do now and pick up from there.

- Everything in this section is covered in far more detail elsewhere in this book. My goal here is to help you to home in on realistic goals for your family, identify key points in the process, and give you some strategies you might use to plan more effectively.

- It's OK if you can't save as much as you'd like to in a perfect world. Winning here is less about giving your student unlimited options and more about setting appropriate expectations with your student—rather than dropping a bomb after they're accepted to their dream school.

## Why saving early matters

One unavoidable rule of all things financial is the power of compounding, and it applies here as well. Simply put, the sooner you begin to save and invest, the more opportunity your money has to grow. More growth translates to larger balances and less need to add more savings.

That means that the earlier you start saving, the more money you'll have available later on and the less you need to contribute overall to have the same balance in the future. Incremental changes can yield big results if you have enough time; with less time, larger changes are needed. A family who wants to have $10,000 per year of college saved—$40,000 total—would get there by saving $100 per month starting when their child is born, and half of that savings balance would come from compound growth—their savings earning money. Delaying that start to age 5 would require saving twice as much each month to get the same balance. Waiting until the child is 12 would require $5,000 per year—more than $400 per month—in savings, and only about $5,000 of the savings balance would come from growth in the account. So the sooner you start, the more work your money does to grow your balance; the later you start, the more work you do.

## Newborn through start of kindergarten

While the college tail should not wag the baby dog, this is the time to get organized. Needless to say, it's all on the parents here. The most important thing is to do what you can, and don't beat yourself up for what you can't. Being intentional about college savings from day one will help you to be successful with those savings.

## Financial tasks

- As early as you can, set up a 529 account for your baby—you can even do this during your pregnancy. Why now, when college is still so far off? Because everyone you know is going to be giving you gifts, and some might be cash. Right now is a great time to start the discipline of contributing a portion of any cash gift to your child's 529 account. Pro tip for expectant parents: You probably have more cash on hand right now than you will at any time for the next 22 years, so this is a perfect time to open a 529 account and make a contribution. (Chapter 5 has additional information on choosing a 529.)

- Set up an automatic contribution to your 529, even if it's just for the plan minimum. Parents of littles have some major financial commitments: Childcare or a reduction in income while one parent stays home, preschool, babysitters, the constant stream of new gear required every time your baby grows an inch taller... not to mention that none of your other financial obligations— mortgage, retirement savings—have gone away. The best way to save for college at this age is to be intentional about it. Recognize that college savings are a priority and automate your savings so that those dollars don't have the opportunity to get spent on something else. Even if you're only contributing the minimum—which is about $15 for most 529 plans—you're still making progress.

- In addition to your automated contributions, make a plan to do the following:
  - Contribute a portion of any cash gifts to your child's 529. If you put just $100 of gifts your child receives annually into

their 529, they'd have almost $4,000 more in savings when they start college.

- If your child's 529 has a gifting page, which allows others to contribute to it directly, make a habit of sharing the gifting page link in advance of birthdays and other gift-giving occasions.

- Every year on their birthday, increase your child's automatic 529 contribution. If you add $10 per month when your baby turns 2, you'll have an extra $3,500 when they graduate from high school. If you increase it by $10 every year, you'll have $22,000 more when they start college.

- If these numbers seem insignificant relative to the cost of college, keep in mind that as the years go by, opportunities will arise to increase your savings *as long as you're intentional in your approach to saving*.

## College conversations

College may seem like a long way off when you're buying diapers, but now is a great time for parents to discuss and get on the same page with their college expectations. Some points for spouses/partners/co-parents to discuss:

- Where do college savings fit in your financial priorities list? Do you have other debts (such as student loans or credit cards) that need to be repaid first? Do you have emergency savings and retirement savings?

- Do you have strong feelings about the type of school you'd like your children to attend?

- What contribution do you see yourselves making to your children's college, and how much (if any) skin in the game do you expect from your children?

- What are your thoughts about college's place in your children's life? Do you expect them to go? Hope they'll go? Not care whether or not they go? I know that most families are in no position to assess their child's academic chops at this point; this conversation is around each parent's expectations for college in general.

## College tasks

- Look up what it would cost to attend each parent's alma mater. The point is not to discourage you; rather, I want you to know early-on whether you should keep buying your team's swag for your kids as they get older.

# Elementary school

Elementary school is a great time to introduce the general concept of college, especially based on your personal expectations for your children's educational path. Chances are, your kids are hearing about college anyway—especially if you attended or live near a D-1 football or basketball school. If they're not hearing about college from their teachers, they're hearing about friends' older siblings' college choices.

## Financial tasks

- If you haven't already set up a 529, do it now! It's never too late to start saving, and if your state offers a tax deduction for contributions, delaying is costing you more in taxes.

- Ratchet up your college savings. Most families' finances get a little more breathing room when children transition from full-time childcare to full-time public school. You may have a few extra dollars lying around each month and at least some of them should be directed toward college. If you increase your college savings by

$25 per month when your child starts full-time school, you'll have another $6,000 in savings when they finish high school.

- This is also a great time to let grandparents and other loved ones know that gifts to your child's 529 are welcome. Or, if your children have grandparents who give generously to their college savings, you might be better off having them open their own 529 account (see Chapter 5 for more details).

## College conversations

Elementary school is a great time to have "why college" conversations with your child. "Why college" conversations at this age start with comments like, "Susie and I were roommates in college; that's how we met." Or "I didn't realize how interesting weather is until I took a meteorology class in college." Or "The first time I went outside the country was when I studied abroad in Greece." Or "I really learned to pick up after myself when I had three roommates in college." The point is to acquaint your child with the concept of going to college and all the interesting aspects of the college experience.

## College tasks

Stick to the fun college stuff at this age. Take your children to visit your alma mater. Go to a college sports event nearby. Many colleges have programs for elementary school-aged children to come for day-long workshops.

# Middle school

Middle school is a good time to introduce the concept of college being expensive and that different school choices will result in different costs. Middle schoolers have probably heard something about how expensive college is and have sufficient awareness of money that the concept makes sense.

## Financial tasks

- Increase your college savings rate. (By now, you've opened that 529, right?) Adding $10 per month in a 6th-grader's 529 will give you another $1,000 upon high school graduation. Bump it up by $25 per month and you'll be closer to $2,500 extra.

- Remind your family and others who might give gifts to your child that they can contribute to the 529 as well.

- Make a projection of what your college savings balance will be by the time your student graduates high school. Assuming you're using an age- or enrollment-based investment, you might guesstimate a 4% average annual rate of return for the next six years when they graduate, plus contributions. Does this seem like a reasonable amount? And by "reasonable amount" I mean an amount that, combined with what you can pay out of pocket and any other resources available to you, would result in your child being able to attend a college? (Not necessarily *every* college.) If not, look at your budget to find some additional cash and start contributing to your 529 account.

## College conversations

Your child may have friends with siblings who are headed to or already attending college, which often sparks some interest in your own household, or offers an opportunity to visit a college. These can be really good jumping off points for a conversation about the fact that your budget for college is not unlimited. Fortunately for you, you've already been coaching your child that "going to college" not "going to [insert college name]" is the goal.

For example, when my kids were in middle school they took a field trip to a local college where a classmate's mother was a professor. They had a great day attending classes and touring the campus and came home very excited about the possibility of becoming Pilots. We talked about what they liked best about the day. (One of my kids: "Having a discussion in class with the professor and the college students." The other one: "The soccer field was really big and they said the stands are full for their games." No twinspeak there!) It was an easy segue from there to a conversation about how they might find those things were available at many colleges, and that we would absolutely help them find and pay for colleges that were good fits, but that our financial resources were not unlimited.

As part of this conversation, you might specifically mention:

- Your in-state schools and even what they cost, especially as compared to private colleges.

- The fact that scholarships are available to make colleges more affordable and that most students get some form of scholarship to attend college.

- The fact that you are saving for college (not necessarily the amount) because it's important to you that your child attends college, and that your savings will be a big part of how you'll pay for college.

## College tasks

- Middle school is a great age to visit a local college or two, or an interesting one when you travel somewhere.

- Look up costs for your in-state public schools as well as what scholarships are offered. You're at a point where it's helpful to have some targets, both financial and academic.

- Use the Student Aid Estimator on the federal student aid website at studentaid.gov. The main reason for doing so at this point is to see if your student is likely to be a candidate for need-based aid anywhere. This tool will estimate your Student Aid Index (SAI);

the difference between a given school's cost of attendance and your SAI is your financial need. Most families are eligible for financial aid *somewhere*.

# High school freshman or sophomore

The rubber is getting really close to hitting the road, and the more you do now, the less you'll be skidding around senior year. Your student will be hearing about college pretty regularly at this point and is probably starting to develop some leanings toward specific schools.

## Financial tasks

- Make a first draft college budget: Savings (divided by 4), amount you can pay from cash flow (parents and student), tax credits if you're eligible, plus any outside help or gifts you can count on. This will help you to get a sense of what's realistic for your family.

- Take a hard look at your college savings relative to some college pathways. Are you saving enough that there's an opportunity for your student to get through college with minimal debt? Pathways might include graduating in three years or attending community college first, but at this point, this goal should be in sight. If not, how might you adjust your budget to increase the allocation toward college? (Hint: If the temptation is to stop contributing to retirement, now is a great time to make an appointment with a financial advisor and ask them to calculate whether your retirement savings are on track. If not, then no, you cannot reduce your retirement contributions.)

- Make sure that your college savings are not invested aggressively at this point. If you're in an age- or enrollment-based portfolio, this is being handled automatically. If you're managing your investments yourself, you should know that the allocation that's appropriate for a toddler is probably not appropriate for a high school student closing in on the college years.

- If family members have told you that they want to help you with college, this is a great time to follow up and get clear about what that help looks like. In addition, remind family members that your student is grateful for gifts into their 529.

- Make sure both parents are on the same page in terms of financial support for college, including expectations for the student's contribution and whether the family is okay with student loans.

- Review the FAFSA formula to see if there are adjustments you can make before your first FAFSA. Your first FAFSA income year is the year from January 1 of sophomore year to December 31 of junior year. See Chapter 4 for more details on the FAFSA.

## College tasks

- Review admissions and scholarship policies at your in-state public schools to ensure that you're on track not just to get in but to get some money. Do the same for other schools as your student becomes interested in them. In particular, look at how the schools value AP or IB credits before your student commits to those classes. Every school will be different, but it's helpful to know if your student is a candidate for schools where these classes are effectively an admission requirement, whether schools give credit for those classes, and whether merit awards are based on weighted or unweighted GPA. (There will not be one consistent answer; many students will apply to schools that have vastly different policies on advanced classes. The main thing here is to make sure your student is not putting themselves at a disadvantage through class choices.)

- Visit some colleges. A great way for young high school students to get a sense of what they're looking for is to visit schools in your immediate vicinity. I think it's even better if you visit some that they're *not* specifically interested in. That lets you focus on the attributes of the school—class sizes, curriculum requirements, academic environment, majors offered, living arrangements and social life, big vs small, urban vs rural—before you (or their friends) start deciding which schools are their favorites. Think of this round of visits as preparing for "real" college visits where you'll go and look at schools your student is genuinely interested in and be able to evaluate them on a set of metrics that's meaningful to your student.

- Take the PSAT as a sophomore. This one is a freebie and will give you a sense of where your student fits in the testing hierarchy, especially relative to merit scholarships they may be eligible for.

- Have your student start a spreadsheet of colleges they're interested in. (There's a template in the worksheets section of Chapter 11.)

## College conversations

This is a great time to start talking specifically about your college budget because your student likely doesn't yet have their heart set on a college that's out of reach financially. Since you've been talking about college all along, your student is already aware that you're expecting them to go, you're planning to help them financially, and that college is expensive and a big commitment for the family. Having done that, you're in a better position to start talking specifics. These can be hard conversations, so it's important to lay the groundwork and establish good communication practices.

One thing I want to remind you: Every purchase you make involves decisions about costs. Chances are, if your kid has a car, it's not a Ferrari. A really important concept in saving and spending is tradeoffs. Saving and spending require tradeoffs because there are only so many dollars available to you and each one can only be spent once. If you spend too much on vacation, you'll need to cut back somewhere else—maybe it's eating out or maybe you won't have enough to save for college and retirement. If you spend too much on college, you'll end up with student loans that restrict your spending choices after college. Using a framework of tradeoffs can be helpful in framing your college budget conversations because it lets you talk about priorities and how to balance them, rather than just being the person saying no.

- Ask your student open-ended questions about college: "What do you think of [insert school name]?" or "What is it about [insert school name/characteristic] that appeals to you so much?" or even "What schools are your friends interested in?"

- Talking about college from the point of view of goals rather than limits allows you to have frank *and positive* discussions about what your family can afford and what you expect from your student: "Our goal is to get you through a public school with no debt, and we have enough saved to do that. You may be able to find other schools that fit within that budget, or scholarships that would give you a wider range of choices." "We're willing to help you find scholarships, but we won't co-sign student loans." "We expect you to be responsible for 10% of the cost of college, whether that means getting scholarships, getting summer jobs, or taking out loans. The school you choose will be what determines how much 10% is."

- Talk about student loans and what it means to have a significant portion of your income going to paying down your debt.

## High school junior

Now is the time to start pulling all the pieces together so that the college admissions process is enjoyable and not overly stressful, so that your student can enjoy their high school experience, too. Your student is probably hearing about college a lot at school these days, so it's important to not overwhelm them such that they come to perceive that their future is more important than their present.

## Financial tasks

- Since you've already talked about budget and expectations, now is the time to start really digging into college costs. Any time your student finds a school they're interested in, use the net price calculator for it (on the school's website) and research scholarships and (if applicable) transfer credit policies. Add this info to the college spreadsheet at the end of Chapter 11.

- Budget for application costs and potential college tours. Between applications, the CSS Profile (if applicable) and sending test scores, you should expect to spend about $100 per college. If your application budget is $1,000, that means your student won't apply to more than 10 schools. Your budget for college tours could vary widely depending on where you're planning to visit, since those could be anything from road trips and staying with family and friends, to air travel and hotels.

- If your student is contributing to their college costs, have them start putting some of their income or savings into their 529 plan. This helps both to make sure the money is available for college and to reduce their savings' impact on the FAFSA.

## College conversations

- Talk your student through the net price calculators for financial reach schools—the schools that aren't quite within budget for you—they're interested in.

- Talk with your student about their vision for their college years and their life beyond that. Are they on a path that is likely to include graduate school? Are they hoping to go "away" somewhere for college? Are there aspects of college life that they perceive as extremely important to their happiness and success? Talking about these things during junior year lets you work together to identify and apply to schools that meet your student's criteria and are within your family's budget.

## College tasks

- Plan some college visits to schools your student wants to apply to. It's fine to do virtual tours if a big trip isn't in the cards. However, it's very important to do the school's "official" tour, which means the student schedules an in-person or virtual tour directly with the school. This will include providing the student's phone number and email address; it is one of the key steps in "demonstrating interest," which is important at many schools.

- As your student gets emails or other contact from schools, they should respond to those they're interested in. Again, demonstrated interest is a piece of the admissions and aid puzzle at many colleges, because colleges want to admit students who are likely to enroll.

- Review the Common App essay prompts to start generating ideas for essays. Students who are applying to multiple colleges requiring supplemental essays might be best served by writing the Common App essay over the summer before senior year.

- As your student builds out their college spreadsheet, they should start including aspects of the admissions process such as whether supplemental essays are required, the school's use of standardized tests, and 75th percentile GPA and test scores for each school.

- If you think you might use an admissions counselor, junior year is the time to find one and start that process. (I'll discuss admissions counselors in Chapter 12.)

# High school senior (fall)

Rubber, meet road. You're here: Applications, the FAFSA, the decision. You know all that, so let me suggest something else: Right now, your child is still in the world of *Everything is possible; work hard and you'll be rewarded*. College acceptances are one of the biggest rewards they've been working hard for. Depending on the schools your student is applying to, there are likely to be some no's coming in the next few months. But you're not there yet. So take a minute to remember that some lucky school is going to get your kiddo for the next four years, and whatever school that is, there is a bright future ahead. Enjoy the last school musical, soccer game, debate, prom—and give your student the space to enjoy senior year, too. Nevertheless, some to-do's.

## Financial tasks

- Complete the FAFSA and CSS Profile, if you're applying to schools that require it.

- Do net price calculators for every school you're applying to. Research each school's scholarships and (if applicable) transfer credit policy for AP and IB classes.

- Finalize your college budget, including making sure that whatever amount you're paying out of pocket is a reasonable sum for your family.

- Confirm anyone else's financial commitments to your student, such as grandparents or others who may be saving on their behalf.

- Apply for outside scholarships.

## College conversations

- For each school your student is applying to, discuss their rationale for applying and the scenario under which they would attend. If they can't come up with one, they should not apply. For example, "I want to go to college in Boston, and this is my Boston safety school" or "If I get the Presidential Scholarship, this school fits our budget and I would accept" would each be a reason a student would choose that school. Chances are, there are not more than 10 schools for which you can come up with a valid scenario in which you'd attend, unless you're applying exclusively to Willy Wonka schools—the schools where your likelihood of getting accepted is about the same as the likelihood of getting a golden ticket to Willy Wonka's chocolate factory—where your rationale might be, "If this is the only school I get accepted at... ."

- Remind your student that there will probably be some no's in the response pile. Even if their rational self understands that dividing 1,600 admissions slots among 25,000 applicants means that many deserving students won't get in, their rational self isn't the only self who'll see a no, and the rejection can be emotional.

## College tasks

- Map out all the deadlines and get them on your calendar. Application deadlines are usually pretty straightforward, but other deadlines matter too: Schools may have earlier deadlines for students applying for some scholarships. Teachers and guidance counselors may have very strict deadlines for letters of recommendation. Every school sets its own deadline for the FAFSA or CSS Profile.

- Decide whether to apply Early Decision or Early Action to any schools and, if so, make sure you can hit the deadlines.

- Once your student has submitted their applications, make sure they check each school's admissions portal to confirm that they have submitted everything that's required.

There's plenty later in the book about what to do once the acceptances start coming in, so keep reading! In the meantime, turn the page for a worksheet on creating your college plan.

**WORKSHEET 3: COLLEGE TASK CHECKLIST, CONVERSATION PROMPTS**

To download this worksheet, go to howtopayforcollege.com/htpfc-book-worksheets.

Regardless of where you are in the process, start at the top and check off everything you've done. (Chances are you don't give yourself enough credit for that.)

# Task Checklist

❏ Open a 529 account for your student (see Chapter 5 for how to choose a 529).

❏ Set up a monthly contribution to your student's account.

❏ Put a reminder on your calendar to increase that contribution by $5 every year during their birthday month.

❏ Set up your student's 529's gifting page and share the link with family and friends who typically give your child gifts.

❏ Look up your alma mater's price: First, check the listed Cost of Attendance, then use the school's Net Price Calculator for a sense of what you'd pay for your child to attend.

❏ Go to a sports or other event at a local college.

❏ Project the balance in your student's 529 account when they graduate from college, based on the current balance, your annual contributions, and an expected rate of return.

❏ Review your household budget to see if there's room to increase 529 savings.

❏ Look up cost of attendance at your in-state public colleges, as well as any merit or other scholarships your student might be eligible for.

❏ Visit local colleges. For children not yet in high school, look up on-campus activities at nearby colleges that they can participate in. For high school-aged students, sign up for a campus tour.

❏ Any time you travel, look up interesting college campuses in the area you'll be visiting and plan a visit, whether formal or just walking around on your own.

❑ Use the Student Aid Estimator on the federal student aid website, studentaid.gov. This will show you the minimum amount you should expect to pay for college on the basis of need.

❑ Review the FAFSA formula (see Chapter 4) to determine whether there are things you can do to reduce your Student Aid Index and therefore the amount of financial aid you might receive.

❑ Draft a college budget: How much do you have saved, and how much could you and your student contribute from your income each year?

❑ Review your 529's asset allocation to ensure that your investments have an appropriate level of risk given your student's time to college. Age-based target enrollment portfolios do this for you automatically.

❑ Ask family members who have said that they will help with college to provide more details around the help they intend to provide. Do they have a 529 established? If so, how much is in it? If not, how do they intend to help?

❑ Review admissions and scholarship policies at your in-state public colleges to make sure you're on track for both admissions and scholarships.

❑ Take the PSAT as a sophomore.

❑ As your student becomes interested in colleges, have them start completing the College Research spreadsheet at the end of Chapter 11.

## Conversation Prompts

### Conversations between the parents

- What are your thoughts about where college fits in our child's life? Do you expect them to go? Hope that they'll go? Want them to decide for themselves whether they'll go or not?

- Where do college savings fit in our list of financial priorities? Do we have other debts such as our own student loans? Do we have emergency savings and retirement savings?

- Do you have strong feelings about what college or type of college you'd like our children to attend?

- What financial contribution do you foresee making to their college education? What skin in the game do you want them to have?

## Conversations with your student

- Mention people or events from your college years or everyday knowledge you picked up in college classes.

- Mention that you've been saving for their college and expect to support them in their education.

- What do you think of [college name]?

- What is it about [college name] that appeals to you?

- What colleges are your friends interested in?

- Our goal is to [for example, get you through college without debt]. We have [for example, saved enough for that to be possible at some colleges]. We're happy to work with you to find ways to create more choices].

- If you took out student loans: Something I wasn't able to do because of my student loans was ____.

- Where do you see yourself at 25 or 30?

## Notes

_____

_____

_____

_____

_____

# CHAPTER 4

# The FAFSA and CSS Profile

## WHAT YOU'LL LEARN IN THIS CHAPTER

How the FAFSA calculates your Student Aid Index (SAI), strategies for reducing SAI, why you should file the FAFSA even if you don't think you'll be eligible for financial aid, and differences between the FAFSA and the CSS Profile.

WHEN MY DAD graduated from high school in 1956, he was fortunate to get an ROTC scholarship that allowed him to go away to college. A year later, my mom had fewer options, so she enrolled in the local public university, lived at home, and graduated in three years.

Had they been born a decade later, my parents might have had considerably more options. That's because 1965 was a big year for education reform. While Vietnam, Selma, the Voting Rights Act, The Beatles, and miniskirts made headlines, education reform was also underway as part of President Lyndon Johnson's Great Society initiative. Declaring that, "For the individual, education is the path to achievement and fulfillment; for the Nation, it is a path to a society that is not only free but civilized; and for the world, it is the path to peace—for it is education that places reason over force." Johnson signed the Higher Education Act on November 8, 1965.[1]

The Act addressed a range of topics related to higher education, including establishment of a Teacher's Corps, and funding for colleges and universities. Title IV of the Act offered a three-legged stool of assistance for students from lower-income families: Grants, part-time employment opportunities, and education loans.

At the signing ceremony, Johnson, noting that less than half of graduating high school seniors enrolled in college, heralded the student assistance provisions: "To thousands of young men and women, this Act means the path of knowledge is open to all that have the determination to walk it."

For the first time, the federal government intended to take a leading role in making higher education available and affordable to American high school students. Because the dollars available as grants and loans were limited, a means for students to apply and a methodology for assessing those applications were needed. Thus the FAFSA, or Free Application for Federal Student Aid, was born.

I bring up all this 1965 stuff because it still plays a role in the FAFSA formula today. I get that probably at least 75% of you picked up this book for an explanation of the FAFSA formula, but focusing your college planning on the formula is like going to the movies for the ticket booth. If you just go for the ticket, you could end up seeing *Harry Potter*, *The Rocky Horror Picture Show*, *Frozen*, or who knows what. The FAFSA is the ticket; what gets done with it is the movie. So before we get into the formula, you need to understand what the FAFSA is and what it isn't.

## What is the FAFSA?

The FAFSA is the Free Application for Federal Student Aid. It is a tool that schools use to evaluate students' financial strength on a consistent set of metrics by calculating an SAI based on the parents' and student's income and assets.* Filing the FAFSA is an annual event for families of college students, starting in the fall of senior year of high school. The FAFSA becomes available October 1 of every year; the due date is set by each school individually. You need to look at the due date for every school you're applying to. For example, here in Oregon, Oregon State's FAFSA due date is February 28, whereas the University of Oregon's due date is March 1.

In turn, the SAI (previously the Expected Family Contribution, or EFC) is a numeric representation of a family's ability to pay for college as calculated by the FAFSA. Truthfully, most people are horrified when they see their SAI because it's almost always far more than you think you can afford. Nonetheless, the difference between SAI and cost of attendance at a given college is your financial need.

This is an important point. The SAI is what the FAFSA or CSS Profile says you can pay for college, and the cost of attendance is—obviously— what it costs to attend the college for a year. The gap between the two is your "need" for the purposes of calculating a financial aid award. That need can be met—or not met—using three types of aid: Grants, loans, and work-study.

The FAFSA is not the tooth fairy. It does not automatically guarantee that college will cost the SAI that it calculates.

In the same way that straight A's don't guarantee admission to Harvard, getting a low SAI does not guarantee scholarships from your school of choice. Similarly, just as straight A's increase the likelihood that you will get into Harvard, implementing strategies that reduce your SAI increases the likelihood and likely size of financial aid awards. But

---

* The Department of Education is in the process of implementing a series of change to the FAFSA called FAFSA Simplification. Those changes are discussed later in this chapter and will be fully implemented by the FAFSA that will be released on Oct. 1, 2023. I am using the new nomenclature throughout this book, including Student Aid Index in place of Expected Family Contribution.

ultimately, those aid awards will be based on each school's financial aid policies and will vary tremendously from school to school.

The FAFSA gives you access to federal student aid programs. These include need-based programs like Pell Grants, work-study, and subsidized Direct Student Loans; and open-to-everyone programs like Direct Student Loans, Parent PLUS loans, and Grad PLUS loans. No FAFSA means no federal Direct Student Loans, no work-study, no Pell Grant. In addition, many state aid programs and some institutional scholarships require the FAFSA for consideration.

## FAFSA basics

At a very high level, you need to know a few things about the FAFSA before even considering the formula:

- You will fill it out every year, for every college student. The FAFSA is the student's FAFSA; both the student and the parent complete their respective sections and sign the form before submitting it. Pro tip: If you have more than one student, you'll want to do all of your FAFSAs in a single sitting. The FAFSA allows you to import parent data from one student's FAFSA to another's, but only in a single online session.

- The FAFSA becomes available on October 1 every year. You do not need to fill it out on that date; each school sets its own deadline for financial aid submissions. However, most students are better off completing the FAFSA sooner rather than later because some financial aid is first come, first served.

- Some private schools also require the CSS Profile, a financial aid form with a slightly different methodology and data set. If you are applying to a school that requires the Profile, you still need to fill out the FAFSA.

- FAFSA stands for **F**ree **A**pplication for **F**ederal **S**tudent **A**id. Note the first F: Free. If you google FAFSA, you are likely to get some results for third-party sites that will charge you a fee to file the FAFSA. Make sure you complete the FAFSA on the Department of Education's website at studentaid.gov.

- Before filling out the FAFSA, the student and parent both need to create an FSA ID. This is not an instantaneous process, so you should plan to do it a few days before you're going to file the FAFSA. To create your FSA ID, simply go to the Federal Student Aid website at studentaid.gov and click on Create Account.

## Why everyone should file the FAFSA

Even if you think you will not be eligible for financial aid, here are five reasons why you should both plan for and file the FAFSA anyway:

1. With some colleges costing upwards of $75,000 annually, many families are in fact eligible for financial aid, even if they don't think they will be.

2. Families in a strong financial position will in some cases benefit in the admissions process by demonstrating (via the FAFSA) that they are able to pay full price.

3. Your financial situation might change. It's nearly a year from when your income—the biggest piece of the FAFSA formula—is counted to when the FAFSA becomes available to file (October of senior year of high school) and nearly another year from FAFSA availability to college enrollment. Much could happen in that time frame, and having filed a FAFSA will be beneficial if any such happening decreases your ability to pay for college. If anyone still thinks change and surprises are unlikely, I'd ask you to go back in time and interview your January 2020 self about what you thought the coming year would bring—probably not a global pandemic.

4. The FAFSA can be a parenting tool. My family has the No Tattoo Rule, which is that as long as I'm paying tuition, no one gets a tattoo. Your family might have similar asks of your student. But chances are, you don't really want to pull the rug out from under your student if they transgress; what you really want is a tool to hold them accountable while keeping them on track to graduate. When I tell my kids that my supporting them through college means them not getting a tattoo while in college, what I really mean is that if they do get the tattoo, the money coming from me will at least decrease and they'll need to take a Direct Student Loan every year. (Psst: If you're reading this before the spring of 2023, please don't tell them that I won't totally pull the plug if they come home with an inked butterfly.)

5. Too many people wait to start thinking about the FAFSA until the fall of senior year, by which time it's too late to do anything meaningful to affect the figures you are entering. Instead, you should start to think about the FAFSA during your student's sophomore year, even though you won't know yet where your student will attend or what your circumstances will be when the time comes to file the FAFSA. This is because, as you'll see below, your tax return income for the year beginning January 1 of the student's sophomore year is the income number that goes into your first FAFSA.

## The FAFSA formula

The FAFSA formula essentially takes account of everything a family might have on hand to pay for college and allocates it into four buckets:

1. Parent income

2. Parent assets

3. Student income

4. Student assets

Similar to income taxes, each of these buckets gets run through a formula and assessed at different rates to come up with an SAI. None of these are dollar-for-dollar calculations. Some items get allowances—like the standard deduction on your tax return—while other items get added back. Some items are based on the present; others on the past.

Here is how each bucket works:

# 1 Parent income

For most families, this is the biggest bucket. And the most complicated.

First and foremost is the "when?" question: Which year of income counts for the FAFSA? The FAFSA uses "prior-prior" year income, but even that term is confusing. Skip the jargon and think of it this way: When you fill out the FAFSA, you'll use your most recently completed tax return. Specifically, if you are completing the FAFSA in the fall of your student's senior year of high school, you are using the tax year that began January 1 of sophomore year and ended December 31 of junior year. If you filed for an extension until October 15, you'll need to wait until your taxes are filed to complete the FAFSA.

(Care to know the "why" behind the term "prior-prior"? If you're completing the FAFSA in the fall of 2022, you're using 2021 income, which seems like it's just the prior year. Prior-prior refers to which tax year is used for which school year. 2022's FAFSA is for the school year beginning in the fall of 2023, thus your 2021 tax data is "prior-prior" year. Anyway, just remember you're using your most recently completed tax return.)

The FAFSA starts by looking at all of your income, taking it directly from your tax return via the IRS Data Retrieval Tool. Then it asks you to add back untaxed income, including pre-tax retirement contributions, HSA (but not FSA) contributions, Roth IRA distributions, tax-exempt interest, and nontaxable pension distributions.

Next, it subtracts a few items, the largest of which are an Income Protection Allowance—a set amount based on family size ranging from around $30,000 up to about $60,000 that roughly tracks the federal poverty level—and federal taxes paid. The result is your "Available Income," which is assessed on a progressive scale (like income taxes) from 22% to 47%. This means that up to 47% of your next dollar earned is considered available to pay for college.

For a very rough estimate of "Available Income," if your family's income is between $50,000 and $100,000 the FAFSA will consider about 15% of income as available to pay for college, meaning you'd be expected to pay between $7,500 and $15,000 on the basis of income; between $100,000 and $200,000, approximately 20% of income; and about 25% of income for those with incomes above $200,000.

## 2. Parent assets

The FAFSA wants to know about all of your non-retirement assets other than your home: Checking and savings accounts, 529s (for all your children, not just the student whose form it is), taxable brokerage accounts, investment real estate, second homes, vested stock options, even farms and small businesses following the 2020 FAFSA simplification. You name it, it's probably an asset. Excluded are retirement assets like 401(k)s and IRAs, life insurance policies, and the family's primary residence.

Unlike income, which is based on the previously filed tax return, assets are valued as of the day you file the FAFSA, so you should wait to file until you've paid your big bills for the month. Assets are counted at net value, so real estate would be worth market value, less outstanding debt and current liabilities. However, outstanding debt with respect to overall assets does not include consumer debt such as credit card or student loan debt; these are not subtracted from assets.

A nominal asset protection allowance (APA) based on the age of the older parent is subtracted from the total value of the assets. Then the resulting number is multiplied by 12% to determine the "Contribution from Assets."

Families with adjusted gross income (AGI) below $60,000 might be eligible for the Simplified Formula, in which assets are not reported. In addition to the income threshold, eligibility for the Simplified Formula is based on the parents' tax return. Specifically, parents cannot have filed any of the following Schedules: A, B, D, F or H, and cannot have Schedule C income or loss greater than $10,000. Basically, that excludes self-employed people, most divorced people, people with passive income such as that from a rental property, anyone who contributes to an HSA and anyone who is collecting Social Security, among others.

## 3. Student income

This bucket includes income minus taxes and is taken from the student's tax filing, if applicable. Earnings from a work-study job are excluded from student income, since they're counted as financial aid. Students receive an income protection allowance of around $7,000; everything above that is assessed at 50%. As with parent income, it's from the most recently filed tax return. Following FAFSA Simplification, students are no longer required to report contributions to their college expenses from individuals other than their parents.

## 4. Student assets

Unlike parents, under the FAFSA students are assumed to have nothing better to do with their savings than pay for college. Thus they receive no APA; 20% of every dollar in a student's possession—bank accounts, UTMAs, Robinhood accounts, and so on—is considered available for college. The 529 provides a way around this—students can contribute assets to their parents' 529s, thus reducing their assets. For example, while $1,000 in a 529 would add somewhere between

$0 and $56 to the student's SAI, that same $1,000 in the student's checking account would add $200. For students with summer jobs who file the FAFSA in the fall, this Contribution from Assets can add quite a bit to their SAI. For more on this, see the "Students" section later in this chapter.

## Adding it all up

Now you've got four numbers: Available Income and Contribution from Assets for parents and for the student.

To come up with the SAI, the parents' Available Income and Contribution from Assets are added (the "Adjusted Available Income" or AAI) and then assessed at progressive rates—like taxes—starting at 22% and going as high as 47% for AAI over $35,100, meaning that every dollar of AAI above $35,100 adds 47 cents to the SAI.

If you've heard that 5.64% of assets are considered available to pay for college, that's what you get when you multiply 12% from the Parent Assets calculation by 47% from the AAI calculation.

Then, this Contribution is added to the student's Available Income and Contribution from Assets to come up with the SAI.

So that's the formula. You can either just punch your numbers into it when the time arrives—or you can plan for it and potentially shave a few thousand dollars off the cost of college. To see how to do that, let's dig a little deeper into each of the buckets.

As you read this, you may be thinking things such as:

- "Small businesses aren't counted!"

- "What about distributions from the grandparents' 529? Don't those go into student income?"

- "Ugh! This is so complicated! We just want to send our kids to college and not pay more than we need to."

If some of this looks unfamiliar or incorrect, remember that FAFSA Simplification was part of the 2020 year-end spending bill. The simplification eliminated a number of questions on the FAFSA and changed a few items. This book uses the data inputs and formula created by FAFSA Simplification, which will be fully implemented in the 2023 FAFSA for the 2024–2025 school year. The key changes for dependent students and how they impact the SAI are detailed at the end of the chapter.

# How to potentially save thousands of dollars (aka FAFSA planning opportunities)

Planning opportunities for the FAFSA depend a lot on your job and family situation. I've broken the FAFSA planning opportunities into a few categories so you can identify the ones that make the most sense for your family. Remember when considering any of these planning opportunities that the FAFSA isn't a one-time deal; you will be completing it every year for every student. Thus you should only engage in planning strategies that you can continue for all four (or more) years.

# Parents with W-2 income (regular jobs)

Unfortunately, changes to the FAFSA over the years have reduced planning opportunities (or loopholes) by quite a bit.

Parents with W-2 jobs have limited opportunities to plan around their incomes simply because they don't control the amount or timing of that income. For example, your employer most likely won't pre-pay your first paycheck of the year so that you get that income in a non-FAFSA year. In fact, most of what you can do revolves around taxes—specifically, paying more taxes in FAFSA years—because the

FAFSA subtracts actual federal taxes paid and an allowance for state and payroll taxes based on your income.

How do you pay more taxes? You reduce deductions. This includes:

• Changing your retirement contributions from pre-tax to Roth. Remember that your pre-tax retirement contributions get added back to your income, so these contributions aren't advantageous in any way for the FAFSA, but they do lower your taxes. A family in the 22% tax bracket who contributes $20,000 pre-tax to retirement annually is increasing their SAI by more than $2,000 due to the tax savings. By contrast, post-tax Roth contributions have the advantage—on the FAFSA—that they increase your current-year tax liability.

• For those who itemize, pull itemized deductions into pre-FAFSA years. This includes paying your January mortgage payment in December and bunching your charitable contributions into pre-FAFSA years. As a bonus, if you use a donor-advised fund in a pre-FAFSA year you'll move some assets off your books, too.

Let's look at a (vastly simplified) example.

Mom and Dad both work. Each has a salary of $75,000 and each contributes $15,000 to their work 401k. Their AGI is $120,000. They don't itemize their taxes, so after taking the standard deduction of $25,100, their taxable income is $94,900. This means they paid $12,285 in federal taxes and they get a payroll tax allowance of $11,475. They have two children—a high school senior and a sophomore—so theirs is a family of four. The family's available income would be:

$120,000 (AGI)

+$30,000 (401k contributions)

−$12,285 (federal taxes)

−$11,475 (payroll taxes)

-$4,000 (employment expense allowance)

-$35,870 (income protection allowance)

=$86,370 (Available Income)

If the family did not have a penny in savings, their income alone would give their senior an SAI of $33,590. This is probably considerably more than they can afford. One of their biggest opportunities to lower their SAI is by paying more taxes in FAFSA income years.

In this case, that could mean changing their retirement contributions from pre-tax to Roth. That's because those pre-tax 401k contributions are reducing their tax bill. If they could switch the full amount to Roth, they would pay an additional $6,600 in federal taxes, which would reduce their Available Income to $75,270 and the student's SAI by $3,102. That extra tax cost might be a stretch, but even changing half their contribution to Roth would reduce the SAI by over $1,500.

Families who itemize have a few additional planning strategies through shifting deductions. This might include prepaying January's mortgage payment in December of the year before the FAFSA income year and accelerating other deductions into the pre-FAFSA year. Think of it this way: Every extra dollar of taxes paid in a FAFSA income year will lower the student's SAI by $0.47. Of course, other items find their way into income, too: Dividend distributions from taxable investments, capital gains, and income from Investment properties or other business interests.

Parents whose incomes vary significantly from year to year may have some planning opportunities to use lower-earning years more than once. Let's say, for example, that your income goes down by 20% from the income year used for the FAFSA to the year when you're actually filing the FAFSA. You can appeal your financial aid award based on the new income data—and then you'll get to use that lower income on the following year's FAFSA. When you file, you have to use the income year requested by the FAFSA; once you've received an aid award, you can appeal it based on the new information. More information on appealing financial aid awards is in Chapter 13.

## Divorced parents

Perhaps the most important aspect of FAFSA planning for divorced parents is that it requires the ex-spouses to cooperate. If you can't do that, planning will be difficult.

The first step in FAFSA planning is determining the custodial parent, since only that parent has to report income and asset data on the FAFSA. This has nothing to do with what your divorce decree says. Previously, divorced parents who shared custody could choose the custodial parent based on which was more advantageous. Now the FAFSA requires the parent who provides the most financial support to file the FAFSA as the custodial parent.

However, it's worth understanding what "providing financial support" means and doesn't mean. This definition is very clear-cut in cases where one parent works outside the home and pays alimony and child support, while the other parent is a stay-at-home parent living exclusively off of that alimony and child support. It's less clear in cases where both parents have jobs, albeit potentially with very different incomes, and no child support is involved. If that's the case, there remains some flexibility in choosing the custodial parent. And it's important to note what does and does not constitute "support." Specifically, owning a 529—even if it's the sole source of the student's education funding—is not "providing financial support" insofar as a 529 contribution is deemed a completed gift to the beneficiary, aka the student.

Some key points in the FAFSA formula for divorced parents:

- Only one parent's income and assets are reported on the FAFSA. However, if that parent has remarried, their new spouse's income and assets are included as well.

- The FAFSA allows the parent paying alimony and child support to subtract those from income, while the receiving parent is required to report those payments among their assets. Often this equalizes income between the two parents to a large degree.

- Only the assets owned by the custodial parent are included on the FAFSA.

- The FAFSA has removed the "Money paid on your behalf" question, which previously required students to report any contributions to their educational expenses from anyone other than the custodial parent. This includes distributions from a 529 owned by the non-custodial parent. This is good news for students with divorced parents where the non-custodial parent owns a 529: There is no need to get into a lot of gymnastics to figure out how to spend down that 529 without losing financial aid.

## Business owners

Business owners have some good planning opportunities for the FAFSA because they have some leeway in timing income and expenses, among other things. Everything suggested here could have an impact on other aspects of your taxes, though, so you should consult with a tax advisor before adopting any of these strategies.

Easy tactics for business owners include pulling income out of FAFSA years and bringing expenses in. If you are used to buying office supplies and other items in December to have them deductible in the current year, you should think twice if you're in the year before a FAFSA income year. Every dollar of expense that gets shifted from a non-FAFSA income year into a FAFSA income year will reduce your SAI by $0.47. Likewise, business owners often defer year-end income into the subsequent year. Again, if the current year isn't a FAFSA year but the subsequent year is, take the income in the current year.

Business owners can also hire their children in the business. This shifts income away from the parent and toward the children, some of whom may not be filing a FAFSA. Even for those who are, the $7,000 student income protection allowance probably leaves them some room for additional income before it starts to impact their SAI. A business owner with two children could hire both of them and pay each $5,000 (assuming they do work that would be paid that much) annually and thereby reduce their own income by $10,000, which would lower SAI by $4,700. This is not to mention that the income gets taxed at the children's rate, not the parents'. Similarly, a business owner with a non-working spouse could hire the spouse in the business. This would not reduce the parents' income or income taxes, but with both spouses having earned income, the family would be eligible for the employment protection allowance, which would shelter $3,000 of income from the FAFSA formula.

# Students

Families tend to overlook their student's income and assets in planning for the FAFSA, which is a mistake.

Now that most families complete the FAFSA in the fall, student assets in particular can trip things up. Consider a student who works 30 hours per week all summer, earning $12 per hour. That student will earn over $3,000 during the summer, with a good chance that a lot of it is still in their bank account when the FAFSA comes out in October. Every $1,000 the student has will increase their SAI by $200.

What can they do instead? If the money is for college, they can deposit it into their 529 so that it becomes a parent asset, meaning only 5.64% of its value is added to the SAI, not 20% if it stays in the student's bank account. The student can also open a Roth IRA to fully remove money from the FAFSA calculation (and get a head start on long-term savings). Or the student can pay some of their own expenses in the fall when things like yearbooks and activity fees are paid. Anything that gets money out of the student's account—even if it transfers funds to the parents—will be beneficial in the formula.

# What about assets?

Parent assets are where most families spend the most time, since by the time you're filling out the FAFSA it's the only part of the calculation you can influence. (Now you see why I suggest planning for the FAFSA during the student's sophomore year of high school, when you can influence the income part of the calculation too. This is a good thing to keep in mind now if you have any younger kids for whom you can start this process earlier.)

Parent assets are counted on the day you file, so make sure you file after paying your mortgage or rent, your credit card bill and any other big bills. If you're planning any major purchases for which you'll pay out of pocket, make them before filing the FAFSA. This might include replacing a car, home maintenance or a new computer for your student. Remember that debt isn't subtracted from assets, so running a balance on your credit card or a home equity line won't change anything in the FAFSA.

Planning your retirement contributions can also help to reduce assets. Families who wait until tax time to make IRA contributions could instead make them prior to filing the FAFSA. Families with large savings accounts could increase 401k contributions to fully fund retirement for the year before filing the FAFSA and spend down their savings account to meet cash flow needs. Then, post-FAFSA filing, they could replenish the savings account because they're contributing less to retirement. Likewise, HSAs can be fully funded pre-FAFSA (though those dollars are added back to income).

People often ask about gifting their assets away to remove them from the formula and having the recipient gift them back after the fact.

This can be quite risky since in order for it to be a gift, *it has to actually be a gift*; if there's an agreement for the funds to be returned, it's a loan or note payable, which is an asset. On the other hand, gifting money to a grandparent so that the grandparent can open a 529 for the student is both a gift and something that you have a reasonable chance of getting back.

## What's the deal with the asset protection allowance?

Every year, every part of the FAFSA formula except the APA adjusts upward based on inflation. This adjustment results in annual nominal increases in the Income Protection Allowance for both parents and students, which should result in a family's SAI remaining more or less the same each year. This is helpful insofar as it lets families know that as long as things remain consistent for the family, so should its access to financial aid. But as mentioned, the APA is an outlier and subject to a different adjustment calculation each year.

The APA has shrunk dramatically in recent years. In the 2018–2019 FAFSA, married parents where the oldest spouse is 50 would have received an APA of $22,300. One year later, that same couple only got $12,500. Think you're mad now? Take a deep breath: In the 2023–2024 FAFSA, they'll get $7,000. In an environment of rising incomes, rising interest rates and a booming stock market, how could this possibly be happening?

To answer that, we need to go back to 1965. That's because despite drastic changes in almost all aspects of our society since then, the rules for calculating SAI are still the ones in the Higher Education Act of 1965. The rules stipulate that the APA:

> "shall be developed by determining the present value cost, rounded to the nearest $100, of an annuity that would provide, for each age cohort of 40 and above, a supplemental income at

age 65 (adjusted for inflation) equal to the difference between the moderate family income (as most recently determined by the Bureau of Labor Statistics), and the current average social security retirement benefits."

Perhaps more importantly, the formula uses a 6% inflation rate and an 8% rate of return for the hypothetical annuity. I'm giving you a big Nerd Alert here—WARNING: There is no way to explain this without getting super nerdy, so get ready.

When moderate incomes stagnate and Social Security benefits increase—the average annual cost of living adjustment for Social Security has been above 2% in recent years—the gap between income and Social Security benefits decreases. This means a smaller annuity would be needed to meet that gap—especially if it returned a guaranteed 8%—so less assets need to be "protected" to ensure retirement income. And therefore, the APA decreases.

If you're wondering why retirement assets aren't included when the formula is all about retirement income, consider this: In 1965, about half of private sector workers were covered by pensions, and exactly zero had 401ks or IRAs—because neither of those existed at the time.[2]

## The CSS profile

The CSS Profile is an additional financial aid formula required by about 200 colleges.

While all schools use the FAFSA to allocate federal funds such as Direct Student Loans, a subset of schools—primarily private schools—also use the CSS Profile in their financial aid calculations.

Think of the Profile as a way for schools to find out if you've stuffed any money into the mattress or otherwise engaged in shenanigans designed to obscure your true financial picture. Because there isn't one SAI formula for the Profile as there is for the FAFSA, you can't tell exactly what your SAI will be under the Profile. You should reasonably expect it to be quite a bit higher.

There are a few key differences between the two forms:

The Profile considers a broader range of assets than the FAFSA. For many families, the most important ones are home equity (although a number of schools have dropped or limited its importance) and non-parent-owned 529 accounts, such as one from a grandparent. Other Profile assets include cash value insurance policies and annuities. Home equity is based on the Federal Housing Multiplier Index, not Zillow or your own estimates.

The Profile includes a mandatory student contribution from income, essentially assuming the student has a part-time or summer job. This typically ranges from $3,000–$6,000, regardless of whether the student has a job or not.

For students whose parents are divorced, most (but not all) schools using the Profile require both parents to report income and asset data. And again, as in the FAFSA, if either parent is remarried, the new spouse's income and assets are included as well.

The Profile assesses income and assets slightly differently from the FAFSA. Parents are given a wider range of allowances against assets, such as for emergency savings and private school tuition, should siblings attend private elementary or high schools, and assets are assessed slightly lower—5% vs 5.64%.

Colleges can include additional questions of their own. These might include questions about the family's cars, how students got summer jobs, whether parents receive any financial gifts, and more.

The CSS Profile's calculation is referred to as Institutional Methodology. This is somewhat misleading insofar as institutions have a great deal of latitude in interpreting the data. For example, some cap home equity at a multiple of parent income. Others factor in regional differences in cost of living. The primary requirement is that the institution's methodology is applied consistently across all students.

A small group of schools use the Profile and FAFSA in what's called Consensus Methodology (CM). These schools wanted to standardize financial aid calculations among member schools to prevent financial aid arms races. Key features of CM are that home equity is capped at 1.2x parent income and student assets are assessed the same as parent assets.

The first F in FAFSA stands for Free. Profile starts with a different letter; you will pay $25 for the first Profile submitted and $16 for each additional school.

Although the Profile is commonly considered the FAFSA for private colleges, remember that it's actually only for a subset of about 200. So before putting too much energy into figuring out the Profile, you should start by figuring out if you even need to file it. In fact, one strategy for saving money on college is to limit your applications to schools that only require the FAFSA.

# FAFSA Simplification

The omnibus spending bill passed by Congress at the end of 2020 included about 170 pages dedicated to FAFSA Simplification. If you want a deeper dive into the ways it changed, read on; if you just want to move onto the worksheet with strategies to reduce your SAI, skip to the end of the chapter now.

## Student income

The FAFSA question about "Money paid on your behalf" has been removed. This means that students no longer report distributions from a grandparent-owned (or other non-parent-owned) 529 as income.

This is a big benefit for students who receive support from people other than their parents.

## Adjustments to income

The Income Protection Allowance (IPA) has increased for both parents and students, though only nominally. For parents it will be based solely on household size and will not consider how many college students are in the family. Allowances for state income tax and other taxes paid (except federal income taxes) have been eliminated. This helps lower-income families and is roughly neutral for higher-income families, since the tax allowance will cancel out the IPA increase.

## Families with multiple students

The number calculated by the FAFSA used to be called the Expected Family Contribution (EFC), and it was an amount the family was expected to be able to pay each year, thus was divided by the number of college students in the family. The SAI, by contrast, is not divided by the number of college students. Under the EFC formula, a family with an EFC of $40,000 total with two college students would in fact only have an EFC of $20,000 for each student. Now each student will have an SAI of $40,000. Again, the impact depends on the family's financial circumstances. Lower-income families will not see much impact from this due to the other adjustments, but middle- and higher-income families with multiple students will see less eligibility for need-based aid. The CSS Profile has not implemented this change, and many colleges that use the FAFSA will continue to divide the SAI among siblings in years when the student has siblings in college.

## Divorced parents

The new formula requires the parent providing the most financial support in the income year used on the FAFSA to be the custodial parent on the FAFSA, regardless of where the student lives. In addition, parents receiving child support will now report that support as an asset, not income, giving it more favorable treatment in the formula. The impact of these changes likewise depends on the family's overall picture. Students who were eligible for aid on the basis of significant differences in their divorced parents' financial situations might lose some of that eligibility.

## Simplified formula

The income threshold for the Simplified Formula—which excludes assets from reporting—has been increased to $60,000. In addition to income, Simplified Formula eligibility is based on tax form status. This has been changed from excluding those filing Schedule 1 (which eliminated eligibility for people with items including unemployment compensation, HSA contributions, Social Security benefits and alimony paid) to those who filed Schedules A, B, C, D, E, F or H. These changes will result in considerably more households being eligible for the Simplified Formula both due to the income threshold increase and removing the Schedule 1 requirement.

## Pell Grants

The new formula expands and simplifies Pell Grant eligibility. Previously, Pell Grants were available to students whose EFC was up to 90% of the maximum Pell Grant amount. Since most people don't know either the maximum Pell Grant amount or what their EFC is likely to be, it was very hard for students or families to know if they were likely to be eligible. Now students will be eligible based on income. Dependent students will automatically be eligible for the maximum Pell Grant if their parents either were not required to file a tax return, or if their AGI was within 175% of the poverty line for married parents, or 225% for single parents. Students will be eligible for the minimum Pell Grant if their parents' AGI is within 275% (married) or 325% (single). Everything about this is helpful.

## Independent students

Numerous adjustments make the formula more favorable to independent students, including increasing the income and asset protection allowances and greater Pell Grant eligibility.

That was a lot! The FAFSA planning worksheet on the next page provides some simple strategies to reduce your SAI, so turn the page and get started.

## WORKSHEET 4: FAFSA PLANNING

This worksheet lists actions you can take to reduce your SAI. To calculate the impact of these actions, please download the electronic version of this worksheet from howtopayforcollege.com/htpfc-book-worksheets.

Calculate SAI from the FAFSA at studentaid.gov/aid-estimator.

Calculate SAI from the CSS Profile at bigfuture.collegeboard.org/pay-for-college/paying-your-share.

## Asset Planning
### Total Assets

Checking/Savings account balances:                            $ _____

529 (all owned by parents) balances:                          $ _____

Other FAFSA assets (brokerage account, net value of
investment property/vacation home, etc.,):                    $ _____

**Total Assets:**                                             $ _____

## Asset Planning Strategies
### Bills to pay before filing

Mortgage/rent:                                                $ _____

Credit card:                                                  $ _____

Car payment:                                                  $ _____

Other: _____                               $ _____

Other: _____                               $ _____

Other: _____                               $ _____

**Total bills to pay:**                                       $ _____

## Retirement contributions

Amount to contribute before filing: $ _____

## Other reductions (example: purchases you intend to make anyway, debt reduction, etc.)

Other: _____ $ _____

Other: _____ $ _____

**Total Assets Removed from FAFSA:** $ _____

---

# <u>Income Planning</u>

Marginal Tax Bracket: _____ %

Pre-tax retirement contributions: $ _____

Amount to switch to Roth: $ _____

## Itemized Deductions to Reduce (only complete if you itemize)

Mortgage interest (1 month, assuming prepaying January): $ _____

Charitable moved to another year: $ _____

**Total itemized reduction:** $ _____

**Total Reductions from Income:** $ _____

# Student Planning

## Student Assets

Bank account balance: $ _____

Student other accounts (Robinhood, crypto, etc.): $ _____

UTMA balance: $ _____

**Total student assets:** $ _____

## Student Strategies

Amount to spend before FAFSA: $ _____

Amount to deposit in Roth IRA: $ _____

**Assets Eliminated from FAFSA:** $ _____

## Assets to Move

Amount to deposit in 529: $ _____

## Notes

_____

_____

_____

_____

_____

_____

_____

# CHAPTER 5

# College Savings Strategies

How to save for college, how much to save, and how to get others to help you save.

WHEN GABI AND I toured colleges, her first reaction to the University of Chicago—I mean from the minute she sat down for the admissions presentation, before they even presented anything—was, "This is the place for me." Everything from that moment forward reinforced that UChicago was her happy place: Small, discussion-oriented classes; a rigorous core liberal arts curriculum that complemented her desire to pursue a STEM major; a residential living experience that seemed tailored to someone like her; a robust theater program. Her heart was set.

When the time came for acceptances and financial aid offers, she received a full-tuition scholarship to the University of Oregon, our in-state flagship public university. It's a great university, but for a lot of reasons, it wasn't a good fit for her. In an "It was the best of times, it was the worst of times" scenario, she also got accepted to UChicago, which on paper is the most expensive university in the world. UChicago also offered her a very generous scholarship, but "very generous" from the University of Chicago was still a five-figure leap, every year, above just the room and board we would need to pay at the University of Oregon. Yet we knew only one of them was the place that felt like her next home. Our savings made it possible for Gabi to choose UChicago, and I'm so glad we could give her that choice.

Saving creates choices. Yet so many people aren't sure how to save, when to save, if they've saved enough, or even if it's worth it to save. If you ever hear the advice, "You'll get more financial aid if you *don't* save for college," I hope a wrong-answer buzzer goes off in your head.

If you don't save, you are limited to the colleges that you can pay for through your income and loans. Some financial aid packages may meet your financial need exclusively through scholarships, but what you think you need and what the FAFSA or CSS Profile calculate you need are often light years (thousands or even tens of thousands of dollars) apart—and whatever the financial aid forms say, colleges are under no obligation to meet your need.

On the other hand, if you save, you're giving yourself and your child choices. If you know nothing else about saving for college, know that. When you save, your choices expand to the colleges you can afford through a combination of spending from your income, savings, and loans—and that's a larger pool of options. Not only that, but data shows that students whose families have saved for college— even very small amounts—enroll and graduate at higher rates than those who don't.

This chapter is all about creating a broader range of choices and improving outcomes for your child through saving. If you do nothing else, follow through on the basics in this first part of the chapter. We'll then move on to look a little deeper at some of the more technical pieces of the savings puzzle.

# How much to save

Too many families get hung up on the calculators telling them that, based on college cost inflation, they need to save perhaps $1,000 per month per child to be able to pay for college.

That's not realistic, and for many families it's so far from realistic that they throw up their hands in despair and quit before they've even started. Don't get frustrated or overwhelmed—just keep reading. The whole point of this book is meeting you where you are and helping you make a realistic plan for *your* family.

Most families use a combination of savings, spending from income, and loans to pay for college. That means the goal isn't to save the full cost of college before your student finishes high school.

As important as college is for many families, it's only one of your financial priorities. Retirement, emergency savings, buying a house, and even just managing a household budget are among the many draws on your dollars. If you don't have an emergency savings fund or you aren't saving for retirement, those need to be priorities *before* saving for college.

# Saving for college vs saving for retirement

So, how much should your family save? Here are my rules of thumb.

First rule: Toss out the saying, "Save for retirement, because you can take out loans for college." That's a significant part of how we got to the point of over $1.5 trillion in outstanding student loan debt. College is one of your priorities and needs to be treated like one. Which is to say, the question isn't: "Should I save for retirement *or* for college?" but "How do I balance saving for retirement *and* college?"

Here's how.

If you are not contributing to retirement at all, you should also not be contributing to college. Instead, any spare dollar you have, once you've established an emergency savings account, needs to go to retirement. College savings should then only be funded through "extras"—tax refunds, bonuses, gifts and the like.

If you are contributing but not maxing out retirement savings—this means contributing at least the maximum annual allowable 401k contribution, currently $20,500 for those under 50 and $27,000 for those 50 and over—then you should save 10% of what you're contributing to retirement for college.

Let's break that down. If you save, for example, $10,000 annually for retirement, you should save $1,000 annually for college. As your savings capacity grows, keep that 10% college savings ratio in place until you are maxing out your retirement contribution (the amounts above). Only then should you increase your college savings rate.

If you *are* already maxing out retirement savings and can contribute more than 10% of your retirement savings to college, how much to save depends on your children's ages and your education funding goals. Young families should target their state's tax-deductible 529 contribution amount, or an amount that will grow to a target annual funding amount such as $20,000 per year (meaning a 529 account worth about $80,000 at high school graduation).

Those with high school students likely have a better sense of their children's academic paths and can set a savings target for a more specific annual college funding level. For example, a family planning for public college might target having enough savings to pay $15,000 or $20,000 annually from savings, whereas a family that is interested in private schools might target $30,000 or more in annual funding (which means you'd need at least $120,000 saved at high school graduation).

There are of course lots of variables that might influence whether or not these targets are best for you personally. These are rules of thumb, not diktats. Parents who are eligible for pensions might not need to max out retirement savings before saving for college. In another scenario, younger parents, specifically those whose children will be attending college while the parents are in their early 40s, will have more time after college to make up retirement savings than those who will be in their 60s when their children finish college. In either case, you might be able to target a higher portion of your savings budget to college knowing that retirement savings will be made up elsewhere— either in your pension or in larger contributions over several decades after your children finish college.

Another rule of thumb: If your college savings balance is more than 20% of your retirement savings balance, you might be overemphasizing college savings and putting your retirement savings at risk. In this case, take a pause on contributing to the 529 while you refocus on retirement. And again, your circumstances may be different, but neither college saving nor retirement saving should come at the expense of the other.

## Where to keep those college savings

Nope, not under your mattress. For the vast majority of parents, 529s are the best place for your college savings.

First, a little background on 529s. These are tax-advantaged college savings accounts established under the Internal Revenue Code but run by individual states. 529 plans come in two "flavors": savings plans, where your contributions earn market returns based on the underlying investments; or prepaid tuition plans, where your contributions grow at the rate of tuition increases in the schools that participate in that plan (more on these prepaid tuition plans later).

Originally intended solely for college expenses, 529 use has been expanded in recent years so that they can now be used to cover some K-12 private school expenses, trade schools, and even to pay off student loans. 529s are a bit like 401ks when it comes to investment choices:

Each plan offers a set investment menu. This menu usually includes age-based portfolios, which allocate the participant's investment across asset classes based on their college entrance date, with the portfolio becoming more conservative as college approaches, and also static portfolios that may comprise one or more asset classes (U.S. large stocks, international stocks, fixed income). There are no income limits on contributions, and aggregate balance limits, while variable by state, are usually well above $235,000.

Most 529s are state-sponsored and offer several tax benefits:

- Many states offer a state tax deduction or credit to residents for contributions. Each state makes its own rules in this regard, including how much is deductible and whether the benefit is per child or per tax return.

- Growth in the accounts is tax-free.

- Distributions are tax-free as long as they're used for Qualified Higher Education Expenses (QHEEs), which include tuition, fees, books, supplies (including a computer and internet access), and room and board. You can also repay up to $10,000 of student loans from a 529, and some states allow 529s to be used for K-12 expenses.

529s have another advantage as well: Unlike distributions from a Roth IRA, which get added back to your income in the FAFSA formula, or from taxable accounts where the gains from selling investments to pay for college will flow through to the FAFSA as income, 529 distributions do *not* get added into the FAFSA and thus do not affect the SAI.

Are you convinced that a 529 is where you want to save? Good. (If you want more options, you'll see them later in this chapter.) Now your next step is to pick a 529 plan, decide how much you can save, pick an investment option, and you're on your way.

# Which 529 plan should you choose?

Choosing a 529 plan can seem daunting because there are so many choices. Each state has at least one plan. Financial services companies like Vanguard, Schwab, and Fidelity each offer their own, and a few private entities offer versions too.

Here's the good news: You can use *any* 529 to pay for *any* college that's part of the federal financial aid system. That includes many international colleges and universities, plus community colleges, trade schools, and more. So choosing a plan doesn't affect your ultimate college choice.

An easy way to get started is this: If your state offers a tax benefit for contributions, then that's probably your best choice. If not, choose one of the low-cost options like Utah's my529 (yes, you can sign up for this even if you can't find Utah on a map) or Vanguard's 529.

If your financial advisor is encouraging you to sign up for a specific 529 such as an advisor-sold plan or the one at their investment custodian, ask them if they get a commission or management fee for your investment there. If their answer is yes, your answer is no. You should not pay management fees or commissions on your college savings. (Fees and expenses are the opposite of helpful to growing your investments.) Instead, choose either your state's direct-sold plan or the Utah or Vanguard plan.

# The best time to start saving

Yesterday, as the saying goes, but it's never too late to start saving. No matter your personal situation, once your baby is born you have a maximum of about 18 years before their first college tuition payment is due. On average, parents begin saving for college when their child is seven years old.[1] This makes sense; it's right around when a child transitions from preschool or full-time daycare to full-time school, so for many families it's the first time they have any financial breathing room.

Unfortunately, waiting until your child is seven means passing up on the investment years that are likely to have the highest returns because of the higher stock allocation in younger age bands of age-based portfolios.

Take, for example, the Utah my529 plan: The age-based portfolio for ages 0–3 has had at least a 1% higher annual return on a 3-year, 5-year, and 10-year basis than the portfolio for ages 7–9. That's because the 0–3 year portfolio is 80% stock, whereas the 7–9 portfolio is 65% stock. A family who is 15 or more years from college can take more risk—and hold more stock—in their college savings than can a family that's only nine years from college. Risk and return go hand in hand, so the riskier portfolio is likely to have higher returns—but would also have larger losses in a down market, which is why the family closer to college doesn't want that allocation or that level of risk.

Fortunately for parents of very young children, 529s can be opened without a big chunk of change, typically a minimum contribution of just $25. Even if you can only spare this small amount, it's a good idea to get started saving as early as you can. A family that contributes just $100 per year to a 529 for 18 years will have over $3,000 saved when their child finishes high school. By contributing $25 per month, you'd have almost $10,000 at the start of college. Contribute $100 per month and you'd have almost $45,000.

And there's an added benefit of opening a 529 for even the most cash-strapped parents: Most allow others to gift to the child's account. So if you really mean it when you say, "Please, no more toys!" you can instead encourage friends and family to contribute at least some of what they'd spend on birthday or holiday presents to the 529. I pitch this split as gifting your child both "fun and future."

If your kid is closer to 17 than 7 and your savings aren't where you want them to be, don't freak out. It's never too late to start. In fact, if you live in a state that offers a tax benefit for your 529 contributions, you can keep contributing all through college and keep collecting free money for college that way. If this is you, now is the time for a candid conversation with your student about the financial guardrails that will need to inform their college application process: How much you can afford to spend annually for college, what is a reasonable amount to borrow, and what other resources might be available to you. (Don't worry, we'll cover this in more detail when we explore cash flow plans in Chapter 14.)

## Making a savings plan that actually *works*

Here's how to get started: As early as you can in your child's life, figure out a monthly amount you can afford to put toward college. That amount may be your plan's minimum, which is typically $15 or $25. Then set up that monthly contribution as an autopay. If you don't want to look at investment choices, choose the age-based portfolio for your child's age. Worst case, you never look at it again and by the time your child is ready for college, you'll have about $10,000 in savings.

You might find that you're like most families and your finances aren't exactly linear. If your child is young, you're juggling childcare costs and perhaps one parent has stepped back from their career for a while. Or your favorite niece just announced she's getting married—a destination wedding the whole family is invited to. Or your kid just made the travel lacrosse team, and now you've got to fit airfare and lodging for lacrosse tournaments into the family budget. That's all just fine as long as you keep your autopay going at some affordable amount.

But good changes happen too: A promotion or bonus, or kids going to school full-time and freeing up money that went to childcare. Good planning acknowledges that all of those things can happen, and it works to minimize the degree to which lifestyle creep is permitted to take over your surplus. You may have heard the phrase "pay yourself first." This applies to college savings as well as retirement savings. When you automate your savings, you automatically remove those dollars from your household budget so they're going to college savings, not Amazon or dinner out. Unfortunately, unlike some 401(k)s that automatically increase your contribution, you have to do this manually for your college savings.

Automating savings also helps to keep lifestyle creep from preventing you from growing your savings. With your 401k it's automatic: Get a raise, and if you're contributing a percent of pay to your 401k you'll automatically be contributing more each paycheck. You need to manually increase your 529 contributions to keep up. I'd suggest that you review your autopay 529 contribution annually during the month of your child's birthday. That's a great time to think about the future you're trying to create for them and make a birthday gift of a higher monthly contribution to support that vision. If you increased your contribution by just $5 per month every year on their birthday, you'd have almost $14,000 more in savings when they finish high school.

Once you've automated your contributions, you can also make lump sum contributions should circumstances allow it. Do relatives give cash gifts for birthdays or holidays? Put some portion of that into the 529. Got a bonus or a tax refund? Make a 529 contribution. Got a little extra cash at the end of the year? Putting some of it into your 529 in December might save you on taxes come April.

Remember that doing something is always better than doing nothing. It's okay to start small—just keep reassessing and know that you'll keep upping your contribution as you go. And since I've rolled through a lot of things here, there's a worksheet waiting for you at the end of this chapter that outlines specific steps for you to take.

Now that we've gotten through the basics, here are some more detailed issues that might pertain to your situation.

# Age-based 529 investment portfolios

529 investments get conservative really fast, meaning that starting to save early is really important. You've probably heard about compounding and seen all those calculators showing the difference in savings needed if you start saving for retirement at 25 vs 45. When it comes to college saving, starting earlier is similar but on steroids. That's because the short time window for saving—18 years—has a significant impact on the ability of savings to grow.

One of the basic principles of investing is that risk and return go hand in hand. In order to get more growth, you need to take on more risk. Generally this means having a higher allocation to stock. In order to protect your principal (the amount you've invested) against loss, you need to take less risk and thus hold less stock. Anytime you're investing toward a long-term goal, you have more capacity to take risk in pursuit of a bigger return when your goal is further in the future. The closer you get to the goal, the more concerned you need to be about loss.

Age-based 529 portfolios are designed to grow when you have the capacity to take risk and then to protect your savings by decreasing risk of loss as you get closer to college. These portfolios start in lower age bands with higher risk, and higher potential for growth investments (mostly stock funds), and then adjust the allocation as the student moves through the age bands to become more conservative as high school graduation approaches. The end result is that once your student is a junior or senior in high school, the likelihood of investment loss is quite low, but the portfolio is also unlikely to see substantial growth. And even if you're not using age-based funds, the same principles of investment risk apply: The further you are from your goal, the more risk you can take. As your goal gets closer, you need to dial back the risk.

In this respect, age-based portfolios in 529 college savings plans are similar to target-date funds in retirement plans: They maintain a risk-based asset allocation appropriate for the amount of time until the goal. But there's a big difference. A target-date retirement fund adjusts from (typically) all stock for an investor in their 20s—who has a 40-ish year timeline until retirement—to around 60% stock and 40% bonds over the course of those 40 years until the investor approaches retirement in their mid-60s. Meanwhile, the age-based fund in a 529 will go from almost all stock for a newborn to almost all bonds in just 18 years. In fact, the typical age-based 529 portfolio for a 12-year-old is more conservative than the typical target-date retirement fund for a 60-year-old.

That means that not only does a late start on college savings reduce the number of years of compound growth, it also decreases the growth rate of the portfolio by missing out on the years of most aggressive growth. A family that wants to cover $20,000 annually for college costs and started investing when their child was a newborn would need to contribute $2,200 annually to have $80,000 at high school graduation. A family that waited until age 5 would have to contribute $3,900 annually—almost twice as much.

If you delay saving, you have three choices to make up for it:

- Save more every subsequent year.
- Take more risk in your investments.
- Plan to have a smaller savings account and thus a more limited set of choices for college.

## Saving *too* much

Nope, this isn't some cruel joke I put in to see if you're still reading closely. For some families, this concern is driven by the moving goalposts aspect of college planning: College could cost anywhere from very little to about $350,000. I'd suggest that you stop focusing on the full range of college costs and instead focus on what you can do, and use that to inform your college selection.

For example, if you're able to save enough to cover $20,000 annually from savings, you can pay another $5,000 annually from cash flow, and you're willing to have your student take out the Direct Student Loan, then you've got an annual college budget of $31,500 for four years and you should be looking for schools that are likely to cost that much. Colleges that will cost your student $75,000 per year shouldn't be on your list of possibilities.

Even so, it's possible that you end up with more money in your 529 than you need, whether because of scholarships or just different choices.

If you do find yourself with more in the 529 than you think your child will need (of course, this falls under the "good problems to have" category), there are many options on how you can use the money.

First and foremost, the money can be spent on a broader range of items than you might think. Not just the more obvious expenses like tuition and room and board (on- or off-campus), but also computers, internet access, and other required supplies. Besides college, 529s can be used for trade schools, some gap years, international schools, community college, paying for the college portion of dual-credit classes taken in high school, and more.

Second, you have options if you don't spend the entire account for college:

- You can use it for graduate school.

- You can name a different beneficiary. If you do this and you are using an age-based portfolio, make sure to change the investment to something appropriate for the new beneficiary. It doesn't have to be the next child—although it does need to be a relative and can even be the parent. In fact, I heard of one parent who named himself the beneficiary of his daughter's 529 surplus. He found a college that offered a PGA golf program, enrolled and used the 529 to take golf lessons.

- You can withdraw the money and pay taxes and a 10% penalty on the growth in the account. There are several pieces of good news in this. First, if your 529 surplus is due to receiving scholarships, the 10% penalty is waived. Second, the withdrawal is taxable to whomever receives it. So a student who's just starting their career and thus doesn't have a high income would probably pay less tax on a distribution than would their parents. Third, there's no requirement that the account be liquidated in any set timeframe, so the surplus could be distributed over several years to minimize the tax bill. Note that any withdrawal is pro rata contributions and growth, meaning that if you put in $20,000 and the account is now worth $30,000, the withdrawal is 1/3 taxable. A client whose son ended up not going to college withdrew $5,000 from his 529 to buy a car that he needed for his job. Rather than complaining about the taxes and penalties, he was thrilled to have about $4,700 for his car.

## Alternatives to 529s

If you're sold that a 529 is right for you, you can skip this section because I'm going to show you why a 529 is a better choice than the alternatives.

If you're still not sure, know it's rare that you'll find another option that beats a 529. That said, I believe knowledge is power, so you may want to read on to learn more about other options—Coverdell ESAs, taxable investment accounts, Roth IRAs, and life insurance and annuities.

## Coverdell ESAs

These are very similar to 529s in that they are tax-advantaged education savings accounts. Sometimes referred to as Education IRAs, in the past Coverdells were a popular option among families with children attending private K-12 schools because Coverdells could be used for K-12 expenses. However, changes in 2017 allowing 529s to be used for K-12 reduced that benefit. (Note: Not all states went along with the 529 changes allowing their use for K-12 expenses. If you want to use your 529 for this, check with your plan before spending the money.) Coverdells have low limits on contributions—$2,000 annually per beneficiary—and are only available to those whose incomes are below $95,000 (single) or $195,000 (married filing jointly). Like IRAs, investments in Coverdell ESAs are self-directed, meaning the investor can choose to invest however they like. However, the low contribution limits make them far less effective as a college savings vehicle.

## Taxable investment accounts

One of the most frequent questions I hear about college savings is, "Why pay the higher expense ratios in 529 plans when there are so many low-cost, tax-efficient investments available?"

It's certainly true that you could construct your own portfolio and then have the added bonus of not worrying about whether your child will attend college or not. However, "tax-efficient" is not the same as "tax-free," and I would suggest that for most families, the benefits of tax-free are greater than the benefits of low expense ratios—even more so when you add in the other benefits of 529 plans.

For comparison purposes, I'll use the Oregon College Savings Plan. It's got fairly average expense ratios for a 529 plan and has Vanguard funds as its underlying investment, but since it only has one investment option per age band, the comparison is more straightforward.

Let's say you have a newborn and you're going to put $4,000 into college savings, right now. You've got 18 years to accumulate, so you want to be pretty aggressive. You want low-cost, broadly diversified, passive investments, and you'll use low-cost exchange traded funds (ETFs) to be as tax-efficient as possible in your taxable account. So you choose to split your investment between Vanguard Total Stock Market ETF (VTI) and Vanguard Total International Stock ETF (VXUS). That's actually a pretty close match to the Oregon College Savings Plan Enrollment Year portfolio for your baby, but without the 0.25% state administrative fee layered on top of the funds' expense ratios.

VTI's expense ratio is 0.03%; for VXUS, it's 0.09%. The 529 uses "Institutional Plus" share classes so their expense ratios are lower—0.02% for the Total Stock Market fund and 0.07% for Total International—but they add that 0.25% administrative fee that we just mentioned. That 0.25% will cost you $10 in performance the first year with a $4,000 investment. So you're definitely ahead on expense ratios in the taxable portfolio so far.

But let's look at the difference between "tax-efficient" and "tax-free." As a tax-free account, the 529 works like your Roth IRA: You don't pay taxes on any growth or income that the account generates on an ongoing basis. Tax-efficient VTI has averaged a 1.84% dividend yield the last few years; VXUS has averaged 2.99%. That means that your $2,000 in VTI will generate $36.80 in taxable dividends in a typical year, and $2,000 in VXUS will generate $59.80. If you're in the 22% tax bracket, those dividends will cost you $21.25 in federal taxes the first year. As an Oregonian, you would pay another 9% to Oregon for a total tax cost of $30.21 annually. Most of us don't think of taxes that way, especially since those aren't paid out of the investment the way expense ratios are. But in this case, the self-directed ETF investments in a taxable investment account are at least three times as costly as the Oregon 529 because of the tax impact.

That's the annual piece. Fast-forward 18 years and it's time to spend the money. Suppose you contributed $1,000 per year and your account grew 5% each year until college. It's now worth about $37,000, so you'll withdraw $9,250 each year for college. 43% of the account balance is attributable to growth. If it's in a taxable account, that means you've got about $4,000 of taxable income each year. Fortunately it's long-term capital gains, so the federal tax rate is 15%, which will cost $600 in federal taxes. We Oregonians will pay another $360 in state taxes. That means that your $9,250 gross distribution is really only $8,290 net of taxes. But that's not all: The $4,000 in gain is also reported as *income* on your FAFSA, raising your SAI by $1,880.

On the other hand, what about the 529? Let's suppose you earned a 4.75% rate of return to account for the 0.25% state administrative fee of the 529. That would result in an account balance of $35,700 at the start of college, so your annual withdrawal is only $8,925. But you actually get the full $8,925. And where does a 529 distribution go on your FAFSA? Remember the secret benefit of 529 plans: *The distributions are not reported on the FAFSA.* So all that tax-free growth over the years has the added bonus of not increasing income for your SAI in the FAFSA, or bumping your income up over the threshold for the American Opportunity Tax Credit (AOTC), or having any other impact on you financially.

All this is before we even factor in a state tax benefit, if you live in one of the states that offers one. In the Oregon plan, $1,000 in annual 529 contributions would get a typical family an annual tax credit of $100. What if you reinvested that $100 into the plan each year? Then you'd have $38,385 in the 529 when college started.

## Roth IRAs

Many families have heard that they should use a Roth IRA instead of a 529 because the Roth doesn't get reported on the FAFSA. That's a little bit like eating sorbet for dinner because it's gluten free—you're focusing on the wrong benefit.

First and foremost, using your Roth IRA for college means it won't be there for retirement. Second, with Roth IRA contributions capped at $6,000 per year for individuals under 50, it's virtually impossible to accumulate sufficient savings for both college and retirement.

Finally, while it's true that the Roth isn't reported as an asset, if you take a withdrawal during a FAFSA income year, you add that withdrawal to your income. So if you saved $10,000 for college in a Roth IRA instead of a 529, your SAI would be reduced by $564 because of your reduced assets. However, withdrawing the money to pay for college would increase your SAI by $4,700. That's the opposite of savings.

## Life insurance and annuities

Unfortunately, the world is full of college "consultants" who hawk life insurance policies and annuities as a college savings vehicle on the basis that they don't have to be included on the FAFSA.

The people who benefit most from using insurance for college savings are people who sell insurance, not parents who are trying to pay for college. There are numerous reasons for this. Two simple ones are:

1.  Although the FAFSA doesn't require insurance to be reported as an asset, the CSS Profile does.

2.  Insurance policies have a built-in cost structure of commissions as well as mortality and expense charges. These increase the cost of the policy and function like an expense ratio in a mutual fund: You don't see it, but it reduces your return. Mortality and expense charges typically run around 1.5% annually; commissions account for 15–20% of premiums over the lifetime of a policy. Picking up that much cost for the purpose of avoiding listing a 529 as an asset just doesn't pencil out. Least of all when the insurance huckster tells you to cash out your 529 to fund the insurance policy, which results in taxes and penalties for a nonqualified distribution.

# 529 savings plans vs prepaid tuition plans

Most 529s are savings plans, where you contribute a certain amount, it grows based on market returns for the investments you've chosen, and when the time for college comes, you have a set number of dollars available to pay. This is like a 401k.

There's also another type of 529 called a prepaid tuition plan. It works more like a pension. With a prepaid tuition plan, you buy tuition credits based on current tuition rates, which are redeemable at future tuition rates. For example, if you put $5,000 into a prepaid tuition plan at a time when annual tuition was $20,000, you would have purchased a quarter of one year's tuition—regardless of what that tuition costs when you actually enroll in college. These plans used to be fairly widely available, but are now much more limited—primarily because the plan provider assumes the investment risk and guarantees you a return.

Prepaid tuition plans have pluses and minuses. On the plus side, your money grows hand in hand with tuition growth, regardless of what markets do. This is great in those close-to-college years when you don't want to take a risk but would like to keep pace with college tuition inflation. There are of course downsides, too, which make prepaid tuition plans more appropriate as one piece of your college savings plan rather than the whole pie. First, they typically have a limited number of schools where funds can be spent to get the plan's full benefit, and if you don't end up at one of those schools you might get a lesser return than college tuition inflation. In addition, most of these plans require you to leave the money there for several years before withdrawing.

Most prepaid tuition plans are run by states and only open to their residents. Another such plan is the Private College 529, which has about 300 participating private colleges.

Once Gabi accepted admission at UChicago, we were able to

contribute during her senior year of high school to the Private College 529, locking in tuition at the then-current rate. With UChicago's tuition increasing an average of 4% every year, this was an easy way to get a guaranteed return on a portion of her college savings that was likely to be higher than what her age-based portfolio in the Oregon College Savings Plan would get. On the other hand, I've worked with clients who contributed to prepaid tuition plans for years only to have their children choose schools outside their plan, and the dollars did not go nearly as far as a savings plan would have.

## How to get the grandparents involved

When grandparents or other loved ones offer to help contribute, first and foremost, make your answer "Yes, please!" A student whose grandparents want to help is going to be better off with that help than without it. There are several ways for grandparents to contribute to college:

- Contributing to the parents' 529. This is often the easiest, especially for grandparents who don't intend to contribute regularly. If it's more likely to be birthday gifts than ongoing contributions, there's no reason to open their own account. Many states allow any contributor to a 529 account to take the tax benefit for their contributions, even if the contributor is not the account owner. If the tax benefit matters, this is something to ask your plan provider. The downside of contributing to the parents' 529 is of course that the account is an asset that is reported on the FAFSA. Nonetheless, it's money the student will have available for college.

- Opening their own 529 with the grandchild as the beneficiary. This is a good option for grandparents who intend to give regularly, especially if they are already gifting to the parents and might be at or near annual gift limits already. And of course, if the grandparents live in a different state, setting up their own accounts may be the only way to get the tax benefit for contributions. Grandparent-owned 529s are not reported as an asset on the FAFSA and, thanks to 2020's FAFSA Simplification, students no longer report the withdrawals as income. However, there is a key difference between the FAFSA and the CSS Profile: Although the FAFSA only asks for 529s owned by the parents, the CSS Profile requires the student to list all 529s for which they are the beneficiary. This means a grandparent-owned 529 doesn't offer as much of a benefit in aid calculations for a Profile school.

- Roth IRAs: While Roth IRAs aren't a good college planning tool for parents, they can be a great option for grandparents. First, these accounts are never reported on financial aid forms because they technically have nothing to do with the student. Second, should the student end up not needing the money (or should the grandparent end up needing it more than the student), it's entirely the property of the grandparent. With retired grandparents, an annual Roth conversion into a dedicated account is a great way to build up a pool of money that is available to the grandchildren for college. Once the student and their family have filed the FAFSA, the grandparents can withdraw from the Roth and gift the money to the parents, who can then use it to pay college bills. Nothing about this transaction is reported anywhere for financial aid purposes.

As a financial advisor I'd be remiss if I didn't remind you that each of these options is something that grandparents should discuss with their own advisors, both to ensure that such gifts are consistent with their own financial plan and because there may be tax or estate planning ramifications.

While any help is better than no help, students are usually best served when grandparents collaborate with parents on college savings. This isn't just about avoiding overfunding; it's about making sure that everyone is aligned on a common set of goals, both sides know what to expect from the other, and ideally, the savings are coordinated to maximize benefits to the students.

I can't count the number of parents who have said to me, "My parents have always said they would help with the kids' college, but I don't know if they've actually saved or how much." If this is you, reach out to your parents right now and ask them specifically what their plans are, what they have saved, and any criteria they have for you to use those savings for your children's benefit. If this is awkward, blame me and say to them, "I'm working on a financial plan for college and my financial advisor needs to know how much other financial help the kids have. You had mentioned at one point that you wanted to help with college. Can you let me know what you are planning in this area? That will allow me to incorporate your contributions into their choices."

Families with multiple children and multiple savers can strategize to minimize the accounts' impacts on financial aid. For example, if parents and grandparents are both saving, the parents could own a 529 for the oldest child and the grandparents could have a 529 for the youngest, thus keeping the younger child's 529 out of the older child's financial aid calculation.

In this scenario, beneficiaries might need to be changed over the course of college, depending on who goes to which college and receives which type of financial aid. Just remember that distributions can only go to the account's named beneficiary. Fortunately, if you need to do so, changing 529 account beneficiaries is very easy, as long as the new beneficiary is also a family member. And most plans allow beneficiary changes to be made at any time.

# I'm sure saving is soooo easy for you, Ann! You're a financial planner!

Okay, I don't love your tone here. To be honest, I know firsthand how stressful it can be trying to put money away for college. My family's savings path meandered quite a bit through the hills and valleys of family life.

My husband works in technology and I run my own business, so our incomes vary considerably from year to year. I stayed home the first couple of years when my twins were tiny, then worked part-time; I didn't go back to full-time until they started middle school. Although we opened 529s when the kids were born, we weren't able to save as much as we might have liked when they were young as we juggled childcare, a twin-friendly car, reduced income, ballet classes, diapers... and keeping twins in diapers definitely isn't cheap. It felt like every time I looked ahead to a cost that was going away, a new one came up.

We didn't really ramp up our savings until I went back to work full-time. We never intended to have the full cost of any college the twins might choose saved in advance; instead, we focused on doing what we could, knowing that this would ultimately inform our college choices. We used our in-state 529, the Oregon College Savings Plan. Lucky for us, Oregon offers a refundable tax credit to contributors to the 529. This means that each of our kids can contribute to the plan and receive a tax credit, in addition to the tax benefits we get for our contributions. The kids literally deposit $150 in December, and as soon as they file their state taxes, they get $150 back. (Now that both are in college, we continue contributing to the Oregon 529 just enough to get the maximum annual tax benefit. I like free money for myself, too.)

Despite our relatively slow start to saving, we ended up in a great place with enough savings that we had a range of choices that worked for us.

Hopefully you have a solid understanding now of why you want to save for college and the best way for your family to do it. Ready to get to it? Turn the page for a worksheet with some immediate steps to take on saving.

# WORKSHEET 5: SAVINGS

To download this worksheet, go to howtopayforcollege.com/htpfc-book-worksheets.

**Do you have access to at least 3 months' expenses in a safe savings vehicle?**

Yes ☐   No ☐

How much are you currently contributing to retirement?

Maximum ☐    Less than the maximum ☐    Not contributing ☐

If less than the maximum, how much do you contribute annually? $ _____

Multiply by 0.1 for your annual college savings budget          $ _____

## Choose a 529

**1. Does your state's 529 plan offer a tax benefit for contributions?**

Yes (Proceed to question 2) ☐    No (Go straight to question 3) ☐

2. What is the maximum annual benefit available?

What is your state income tax rate?                        _____

How much do you plan to contribute annually?          $ _____

Calculate your tax benefit: If less than the maximum eligible amount, multiply contribution x state income tax rate. If more than the maximum, multiply the maximum x state income tax rate.                        $ _____

3. If your state does not offer a tax benefit:

Will your initial deposit be more than $3,000?

Yes ☐   No ☐

If yes -> Vanguard

If no -> Utah's my529

First-year monthly contribution amount    $ _____

Total first-year contribution    $ _____

Month to adjust contribution    $ _____

Monthly goal after next adjustment    $ _____

## Task Checklist

❑   Open account

❑   Set up monthly contribution

❑   Choose investment portfolio

❑   Note in calendar for annual increase

## Notes

_____

_____

_____

_____

_____

_____

_____

_____

# CHAPTER 6

# Different Types of Scholarships

## WHAT YOU'LL LEARN IN THIS CHAPTER

What types of scholarships are available, who gets scholarships, how financial aid is packaged.

ALEX IS LIVING testimony to the fact that there's a scholarship for every student. The same effort his twin sister put into academics, he put into pursuing his own path. He chose a soccer club that no one else from his high school played for, spent his summers at a camp his friends didn't go to, even dated a girl from another high school.

So when the time came to apply to colleges, he was not especially enthusiastic about staying in-state. Our mandate was that, given how little emphasis he had put on high school academics—his GPA was below 3.5—we were not going to pay more than in-state costs for his college.

Rather than take that lying down, he decided to research his options. He realized that one of the schools he was interested in, the University of Arizona, had a merit scholarship just for him: a student with OK grades and strong test scores. He applied, was accepted with the scholarship, and has been kicking butt in college in a way that I don't think he would have had he followed his high school friends to the University of Oregon.

Maybe it's the sappy letter I left in his dorm room with a copy of *The Road Less Traveled* when we dropped him off freshman year that motivated him? He's not only in budget and in his happy place—he has also been incredibly successful academically. Daily I debate reaching out to his high school math teacher, who seemed convinced he'd never amount to anything, to mention that he's tutoring statistics in college.

That's a different topic. The topic of this chapter is scholarships: How they work and how to get them.

## How to use scholarships in your college plan

Before we get too far, I want to make one thing clear:

Scholarships are a tool to bring your college costs in line with your budget.

The way you use scholarships in your planning is this: When you find schools that you're interested in, you research their financial aid and scholarship policies and determine whether you are likely to get enough aid for that school to fit into your budget. This includes doing the net price calculator, most of which focuses primarily on need-based aid, and researching merit awards offered by the school. Around two-thirds of students receive some form of scholarship or financial aid, and about 100% of students are eligible for some form of aid, somewhere. It's up to you to find out where you're likely to get scholarships.

So, what are those scholarships, and where do they come from?

# Three types of scholarships

The federal government is the largest provider of financial aid overall, disbursing over $120 billion annually in student aid.

However, on just about every college campus, the school itself is the biggest source of aid, with institutional awards typically being far more generous than federal awards. About two-thirds of students receive some form of grant or scholarship aid. Since institutional generosity is what drives cost differences between schools, I'm going to focus on institutional aid rather than federal.

Scholarships fall into three categories:

- Financial aid, which is disbursed on the basis of need and is generally referred to as grants in an aid award.

- Institutional merit scholarships, which are awarded to students the school hopes to attract and enroll; typically, if your child falls above the 75th percentile academically, they can expect merit aid from schools that grant it.

- Outside scholarships, which are offered by third parties that are generally unaffiliated with the school itself.

## Financial aid

Financial aid often combines institutional and federal funds. Aid awards are based on the FAFSA or CSS Profile and cannot exceed the student's need as calculated by the applicable aid form.

 Important: While the aid total cannot exceed a student's need, schools are under no obligation to *meet* the student's need. Thus, while the FAFSA is important, each school's aid policies will be far more important in determining the student's net cost to attend.

A small number of schools meet 100% of demonstrated need through grants and scholarships alone; an even smaller number are completely free or tuition-free to students with family income below certain thresholds. (Don't worry, I'll tell you how to find those schools when we look at researching colleges in Chapter 11.)

Most schools use a combination of grants, loans, and work-study to meet need. Since financial aid is based on the FAFSA or Profile, the student will get a new package every year based on that year's FAFSA.

## Institutional merit aid

Institutional merit scholarships tend to be the most generous. Since the school is spending its own money, it can award scholarships based on its own priorities.

As with financial aid, not all schools offer merit scholarships: The Ivy Leagues and other extremely selective schools rarely offer merit awards. However, outside of that band of colleges, students are likely to find many extremely generous schools, such that it's not unreasonable to expect that you might attend a private or out-of-state public school for about the same cost or even less than in-state public.

It may come as a surprise to families who have only heard about schools with single-digit acceptance rates that, in fact, most colleges are actively seeking to admit and enroll students and will gladly shell out some cash to get students to attend.

## Outside scholarships

Outside scholarships are the final type of scholarship. These come from a variety of sources: employers, civic or community organizations, interest groups, and so on.

While you can certainly Google "college scholarships for [your student's attribute]" or go to fastweb or any of the other online scholarship databases to see thousands of available scholarships, the best sources of outside scholarships are likely to be closer to home.

That's because a national scholarship will attract tens of thousands—if not hundreds of thousands—of applications, but local organizations offering scholarships attract far fewer applicants and thus are somewhat more attainable.

Furthermore, many of these local organizations already know the student so they're looking at the full package, not just a short essay or a GPA. Employers, club sports, civic organizations and more offer college scholarships. My daughter found a wonderful scholarship through her high school computer science teacher. In addition to an annual scholarship, she's also received a computer, money for computer supplies, and a professional mentor who helped her find a summer internship.

Outside scholarships are generally smaller than institutional awards but can make a meaningful difference in a student's cost of attendance. However, schools are required to count outside scholarships as student income when calculating a financial aid package, so often these scholarships end up being worth less than they seem to be.

## Building a financial aid package

Financial aid and merit scholarships are often combined in the same package. When a school offers both, it's common for a student to receive both. And they may combine in interesting ways: My daughter received an award at one school that included a Direct Student Loan and a merit award in the amount of the Direct Student Loan, effectively offsetting the student loan every year.

Federal and state financial aid grants are limited. Most students with high need will be best served by colleges that are generous with institutional need-based aid. Federal financial aid is a three-legged stool of grants, loans, and work-study. The primary free money from the federal government for undergraduates is the Pell Grant, which is available to students from families with incomes up to either 175% or

225% of the federal poverty level. However, at about $6,500, the Pell Grant doesn't come close to covering college costs.

Some states offer their own aid programs, ranging from free community college for all, to grants for students with financial need. Each state sets its own policies in this area. To find out yours, Google "[state] student access (or aid) commission."

State grants can be especially valuable for students in high-cost-of-living states where their income is unlikely to qualify for federal grants. However, most states restrict use of these grants to in-state schools, and like Pell Grants, they help but typically don't cover the full cost of tuition, let alone room and board, books, etc.

Colleges will automatically apply Pell Grants to eligible students' financial aid packages, then layer federal and state programs with their own institutional aid such that a student receiving a Pell Grant or a state grant might be eligible for institutional aid in addition to those awards.

Financial aid is reasonably straightforward: The school applies its aid policies to the student's SAI as calculated by the FAFSA or Profile and generates an award. But merit is far more opaque, so let's spend some more time there.

## Merit scholarships

Who gets merit scholarships?

If you answered "athletes," here's some news: The pool of academic scholarship dollars dwarfs that of athletic scholarships. Yep, mathletes usually receive larger scholarships than athletes do.

Merit scholarships are the primary means of tuition discounting and they're broadly available. A few key points about merit scholarships:

- Test scores are still important. Test-optional admissions is probably here to stay, but that doesn't mean colleges won't continue using test scores to dole out merit aid.

- Unweighted GPAs matter. Many schools award merit on the basis of unweighted GPA. Thus, students should consider whether they are likely to earn the same letter grade in a weighted (AP/IB/dual-credit) course as they would in a standard course. Of course this is a separate consideration than admissions; many of the most selective colleges essentially require a student to have a full slate of advanced courses to be considered for admission. Then again, those schools don't offer merit aid.

- Public colleges offer merit awards. There's a common misperception that merit aid is the realm of private colleges. In fact, many—if not most—public colleges offer it as well, in many cases with the goal of attracting out-of-state students. And many public colleges participate in regional tuition exchanges, where students in nearby states can attend at a discount from the usual out-of-state tuition rate. Chapter 11 has more information on regional tuition exchanges.

- Merit aid is often offered on the basis of non-academic qualifications. While you might be thinking "sports," you should instead be thinking "unique qualities." This might include athletic abilities, but it might also include factors such as being the only student from a specific state in that year's applicant pool.

To understand academic merit scholarships, it's helpful to detour to the *U.S. News & World Report* college rankings.

There's a great deal of pearl-clutching around these annual rankings, especially among the ranks of educational pundits who rightly point out that the ranking system is heavily tilted toward wealthy schools, the methodology is flawed, and that the rankings have a far greater weight in the world of public opinion than they deserve.

Schools have a love-hate relationship with the rankings, too—and not just that they love receiving high ratings and hate low ones. While they may decry the same systemic flaws as the pundits, schools also issue press releases trumpeting their rankings and offer incentives to students and sometimes even faculty in order to improve their standing.

Why do you care about this? Because merit scholarships that bring in higher-achieving students are a primary tool that schools use to move up in the *U.S. News* rankings.

*U.S. News* tweaks their formula periodically, but the primary components are fairly consistent. Two are based on the student body: Outcomes, which currently accounts for 35% of the ranking; and Student Excellence, which counts for 10%.

Outcomes include graduation and retention, graduation rate performance (measuring actual vs predicted graduation rate) and social mobility, measuring a school's ability to retain and graduate Pell Grant recipients.

Student excellence is based on test scores and high school class rankings of the student body. I predict that many of you are thinking, "But wait! I thought most schools are test-optional." Even in the 2020–2021 admissions cycle, when the SAT and ACT were barely available to be taken, about half of students submitted test scores.

(Trivia question: Why do so many schools issue press releases about their low acceptance rates? Because in 2018, *U.S. News* dropped selectivity from its ranking criteria, so now the schools have to promote their selectivity themselves.)

Let's take a moment to acknowledge that it's unfortunate that there is a ranking system that leads to specific college behaviors that have nothing to do with educating students. Done.

Now let's talk about why this is in fact wonderful. Colleges want to be ranked higher. One way to rank higher is to admit more students with strong academic records. Therefore, high school students who would improve a college's rating are likely to be offered financial incentives (aka scholarships) to attend that college. Typically, if you fall above the 75th percentile academically, you should expect merit aid if the school grants it.

Many schools go a step further and offer specific scholarships to all applicants whose GPA and test scores exceed certain thresholds. Unfortunately, we are trained to think that acceptance to an academic "reach" school is the best possible college outcome. Please retrain yourself to think that your academic reach school will probably be your most expensive option. Instead, the further right on the academic profile bell curve your student is, the more likely they are to get a large scholarship. (We'll talk about how to find these schools when we look at researching colleges in Chapter 11.)

There's a second reason that merit scholarships are so popular: As I've mentioned, most colleges are actively trying to recruit and enroll students. This may sound crazy when you keep hearing about single-digit acceptance rates, but hundreds of colleges every year extend their admission deadlines past May 1 for this reason. And plenty of schools, especially public ones, keep their admission open all summer simply to be of service to the population they're hoping to educate. Remember supply and demand from economics? Offering scholarships is a means of bending the demand curve to meet the available supply. Which begs the question, why not just lower prices? Easy answer: Far too many families are willing to pay full price. Why should a college give up charging high tuition rates when one-third or more of students are willing to pay them?

While the bulk of merit money is distributed based on grades and test scores, many schools offer awards based on extracurriculars, leadership, community service, excellence in certain areas, and even specific interests. Some merit aid is awarded automatically, while other scholarships require an application—particularly those based on non-academic attributes or accomplishments. Again, it's up to each school to set its priorities and processes for accessing scholarships.

Most public colleges offer merit aid—and not just to in-state students. One of the best things about public schools' merit awards is that many are awarded automatically on the basis of grades and test scores—no additional application required.

This allows students and families to research scholarship policies at their in-state schools well in advance of applying and know what grades and test scores are needed to get them.

For example, if your in-state school of choice offers $5,000 annually for an unweighted high school GPA of 3.6 or higher and your student is struggling in AP chemistry, they might benefit from switching to regular chemistry if that means they're likely to earn a higher grade. Likewise, if your student's practice SAT or ACT scores show they're a little below a scholarship threshold, investing a few hundred dollars in some test preparation to bring scores up might pay off thousands.

## Athletic scholarships

What about student athletes? Isn't athletic ability the ticket to free college? With apologies to parents of star soccer players or track athletes, no.

Athletic scholarships are in fact quite limited; most student athletes will find that their athletic achievements are far more beneficial in the admissions process than in getting scholarships. In fact, according to the National Collegiate Athletic Association (NCAA), only about 2% of high school athletes will get athletic scholarships. The NCAA has strict rules for athletic scholarships and for student athletes to receive other scholarships. The next chapter has additional detail about athletic scholarships.

# Yield and selectivity

To understand scholarships, it's helpful to understand the concepts of selectivity and yield.

Selectivity is pretty straightforward, especially since colleges issue press releases about it. It's the rate at which applicants are admitted to colleges. Schools like Stanford and Harvard admit fewer than 10% of applicants in a typical year. While a handful of top schools admit single-digit percentages of applicants, colleges ranking among the 100 most selective admit up to 30% of their applicants annually.

How do schools become more selective? They can either increase their applicant pool (admitting 4,000 students from a pool of 10,000 applicants is a 40% acceptance rate, but admitting 4,000 out of a pool of 40,000 is 10%) or they can increase their yield (the number of admitted students who enroll), thus allowing them to admit fewer students. Most schools trying to become more selective actually try to do both.

Yield, the percent of admitted students who enroll, is a huge driver of selectivity. Let's say a college's yield is 25%, which is fairly typical. That means 25% of admitted applicants enroll, so they need to admit four students to enroll one. Willy Wonka schools—the colleges where getting in is about as likely as getting a golden ticket to the chocolate factory—on the other hand, have yields in excess of 80%. That means that more than 8 out of 10 accepted students enroll. If you're trying to fill a freshman class of 2,000 students and you're a typical college with a 25% yield, you need to admit 8,000. If you're Stanford, you only need to admit 2,500. Even if both schools got the same number of applicants and ended up with the same size class, Stanford would be more selective because it would need to admit far fewer students.

Increasing scholarships increases yield because it shifts the demand curve by lowering the price (remember Econ 1?). That means, if a student is accepted to two comparable schools but one costs $10,000 less than the other because of scholarships, odds are good that they'll choose the less expensive school, thus increasing the demand, enrollment and yield.

When you think of the college admissions process, it can be helpful to think about it from the perspective of the admissions office, which is trying to both get students to apply, and get those who've applied to accept admission. Scholarships help in both of those categories, and that's a big part of why scholarships are so broadly available.

# Aid packaging

Aid packaging is the process where a college assembles a financial aid package for a student. Financial aid packages can include loans and work-study in addition to grants and scholarships; many include a combination of merit and need-based awards. The important take-aways are:

- The same amount of scholarships can result in different net costs.

- The same bottom-line cost on a financial aid award letter can be very different depending on the actual aid package.

## Where colleges' money comes from

Before we get into aid packaging, it's helpful to understand where colleges' money comes from. Colleges get most of their money from one or more of three sources: state budgets, endowments, and tuition.

Aid packaging philosophies follow from there. Colleges with large endowments have considerably more ability to discount tuition because tuition is a smaller piece of their overall financial picture. And those funded primarily through tuition have far less ability to discount tuition because tuition itself is their primary funding source. State schools, on the other hand, tend to rely on federal programs such as Pell Grants and Direct Student Loans to meet financial need.

And of course, aid dollars are allocated based on the institution's priorities. A school that wants to move up in the *U.S. News & World Report* college rankings will allocate its dollars toward high-achieving students. A school wanting to diversify its student body might focus its aid budget on students with financial need. Many public schools offer merit scholarship programs reflecting state priorities, such as keeping high-achieving students in-state or increasing out-of-state enrollment.

## Aid packaging in action

Colleges can include federal aid programs as well as their own scholarships in an aid package. While federal aid is allocated on the basis of need and has allocation rules that schools are required to follow, institutional aid is awarded at the discretion of the school. Different schools place different values on different student attributes, so it's reasonable to assume that the same student will see a different net cost at every school they're accepted to.

By way of example, Gabi received the following award offers, each from a different college:

- Full-tuition merit scholarship.

- Merit award of $2,500; $37,000 institutional grant.

- Merit award of $8,000.

- Merit award of $10,000; additional merit award in the amount of the federal Direct Student Loan; $15,000 grant.

- Merit award of $10,000.

Clearly, she was more attractive to some schools than to others, with her net costs after these awards ranging from $12,000 to $68,000. Her choices included an in-state and out-of-state public school and several private schools, so overall cost of attendance ranged from around $26,000 to $82,000. Other schools she was interested in indicated via their net price calculators that she would not receive any aid. Knowing what her budget was, she didn't apply to any schools for which that was the case.

Every school is required to have a net price calculator, which is a tool that families can plug their financial—and sometimes academic—data into and get an estimate of the financial aid and scholarships they are likely to receive. More on these in Chapter 11.

Besides grants, loans, work-study and scholarships, schools also factor outside scholarships into their aid packages. In fact, the Department of Education requires outside scholarships to be considered when federal aid funds other than Pell Grants are part of a student's package, and most schools follow that logic when offering institutional funds as well.

What does this mean in practice? First and foremost, need-based financial aid will be reduced by 50% of the value of the outside scholarship (more on that below). Typically an outside scholarship is disbursed directly to the school and credited to the student's account. Whether or not that's the case, students are required to report outside scholarships to the school.

Schools can determine how to package outside scholarships within their overall financial aid framework, so students may see very different outcomes with different schools. When an aid package includes work-study, a subsidized loan, and an institutional grant, the school decides which portion of the aid package to credit the outside scholarship against.

One student I worked with, who attends a 100% need-met/no loans school, received a $30,000 institutional grant and a $5,000 outside scholarship. Her institutional grant was reduced by $2,500 as a result of the outside scholarship. She still came out ahead by $2,500, but she chose to focus on working over the summer before college rather than applying for some other smaller scholarships since the summer job would have less impact on her financial aid.

Another student received a $15,000 outside scholarship. Her financial aid package included work-study and a subsidized loan in addition to a grant. That school's policy was to reduce the work-study and subsidized loan first. That accounted for $6,500 of the outside scholarship; her institutional grant was reduced by 50% of the remaining scholarship balance, or $4,250. The lost loan subsidy would cost around $720 over four years, so she still came out ahead by about $10,000.

Scholarships can clearly make the difference between an affordable college and an out-of-reach one. Now turn the page for a planning worksheet to see what scholarships you may be eligible for.

## WORKSHEET 6: MERIT AID PROFILE

To download this worksheet, go to howtopayforcollege.com/htpfc-book-worksheets.

### Academics

Student's weighted GPA:

_____

Unweighted GPA:

_____

Student's Test Scores:

_____

SAT Verbal:

_____

SAT Math:

_____

ACT:

_____

### Classes and Extracurriculars

| Class/Extracurricular | Honors/Awards | Person to ask about scholarships |
|---|---|---|
| 1 | | |
| 2 | | |
| 3 | | |
| 4 | | |
| 5 | | |

## Merit Awards at In-State Colleges

| College | Scholarship Name/ Amount | Minimum GPA | Application Required? |
|---|---|---|---|
| 1 | | | |
| 2 | | | |
| 3 | | | |

## Colleges Where My Student Is in the Top 25% Academically

| College | Offers Merit Scholarships? | Scholarship Application Process |
|---|---|---|
| 1 | | |
| 2 | | |
| 3 | | |

## Colleges in My Student's Regional Tuition Exchange

| Name of College | Application Process |
|---|---|
| 1 | |
| 2 | |
| 3 | |

## Scholarships offered by parents' employers

| Scholarship | Amount | Application Process |
|---|---|---|
| 1 | | |
| 2 | | |
| 3 | | |

## Local Scholarships I'm eligible for (your college and career center has a list)

| Scholarship Name | Amount | Application Process | Application Due Date |
|---|---|---|---|
| 1 | | | |
| 2 | | | |
| 3 | | | |

## National Scholarships I'm eligible for (Use fastweb, scholly, etc.)

| Scholarship Name | Amount | Application Process | Application Due Date |
|---|---|---|---|
| 1 | | | |
| 2 | | | |
| 3 | | | |

# CHAPTER 7

# Student Athletes

## WHAT YOU'LL LEARN IN THIS CHAPTER

Who gets athletic scholarships, what levels of athletic competition are available, admission and merit scholarship opportunities for athletes.

DURING ALEX'S JUNIOR year of high school, he played for a club soccer team that was very focused on getting the players onto college teams. Wherever they traveled, they visited local colleges, toured the campus and met with coaches and players. Alex's conclusion from those visits was that he wasn't interested in going to a college where he would be able to play soccer. Now he's a dedicated intramural athlete, content with starring on the Microwaves—his intramural team—in indoor and outdoor soccer and knocking it out of the park in kickball. But plenty of his high school and club teammates are now playing college soccer, at every available level.

Only about 6% of high school athletes continue playing at the collegiate level; less than 2% earn athletic scholarships. With over 8 million high school athletes, that means about 160,000 athletic scholarships, and a 98% chance that your student athlete won't be getting one. By contrast, there are colleges where 98% or more of students receive a merit scholarship.

Student athletes wanting to pursue their sport at the collegiate level should start by thinking about why, because that will help to frame the college search. Are they hoping to compete professionally or at the Olympic level? Is the goal scholarship money or getting a leg up in admission to highly selective colleges? Are they someone who engages with their environment through sports, who sees continued participation as a way to make friends and find their place in new surroundings? How important is playing time vs level of competition? Different colleges, and different search strategies, will meet different goals.

Colleges offer a huge range of options for students to participate in athletics. In addition to traditional varsity sports, many offer highly competitive club programs that compete regionally and even nationally. Club teams at Division-1 colleges are often filled with students who had offers to play at the Division-2 or -3 level, which can be great options for students who want to continue to engage through sport but don't want a varsity-level commitment.

Student athletes should also research the recruiting assistance available to them and make sure they are availing themselves of all available resources, whether through club sports, coaches, their high school, or private counselors. In addition to finding schools that fit them as students, athletes need to know whether that school's team needs someone in their position.

## So, how do athletic scholarships work, and who gets them?

First and foremost, college sports are segmented into two groups for scholarship purposes: "headcount" sports—where there is a set number of scholarships and roster slots for each team, and every athlete receives a full scholarship—and "equivalency" sports, where each team gets a set number of scholarships to be allocated at the coach's discretion among as many players as they want. Headcount sports are the sports that usually earn the most money: D-1 men's and women's basketball, men's football, and women's volleyball, gymnastics, and tennis. All other D-1 sports, and *all* D-2 sports, are equivalency sports. D-3 schools do not offer athletic scholarships.

For example, soccer—men's and women's—is an equivalency sport. Men's D-1 soccer teams get 9.9 scholarships, while they may roster 25 student athletes. Assuming that a handful of players get full scholarships, coaches need to be pretty creative when divvying 4.9 scholarships among 20 student athletes.

In equivalency sports, larger scholarships go to student athletes who can generate results at the conference level. So having the fastest 100 meter time in your state doesn't mean as much for scholarships as where that time puts you among Pac-12 or SEC or Big 10 times. And of course, coaches are assembling teams and teams may be overstocked in certain positions. If your top choice college already has multiple scholarship athletes in your position, they might not be adding any more.

In all, athletes don't get nearly as much scholarship money as mathletes. In the 2019–2020 school year, just over $4 billion in athletic scholarships was disbursed, with the vast majority—$2.76 billion—being at the D-1 level. By contrast, more than $13 billion was awarded in academic merit scholarships.

At the D-3 level, where no athletic scholarships are offered, many student athletes instead receive academic merit scholarships at the discretion of the school. Especially in equivalency sports, many student athletes choose to enroll and compete at D-3 colleges because of the larger merit scholarships they receive.

# What about admissions?

Many student athletes use their athletic abilities to improve their admission chances at highly selective schools. At MIT, for example, almost a quarter of students are varsity athletes. College coaches are allowed to recommend student athletes for admission; this is the source of the Operation Varsity Blues scandal, where a college consultant took bribes from wealthy parents to get coaches to admit their children as "student athletes," even if the student had no experience in the sport.

At the most selective schools, just being a good athlete isn't enough; the student also needs to meet the college's academic requirements. The Ivy League, for example, has an "academic index" for student athletes to ensure that admitted athletes' academic qualifications—GPA and test scores—do not differ substantially from those of the student body as a whole. While Ivy League colleges do not offer athletic scholarships, they do offer athletes who are also excellent students a higher likelihood of admission.

Grades are important for student athletes for multiple reasons. First and foremost, the NCAA sets minimum GPA thresholds for student athletes to be eligible to participate in their sport. Second, in order to prevent schools from simply offering merit aid to all student athletes to circumvent athletic scholarship restrictions, the NCAA has strict rules about student athletes receiving merit aid. In addition to minimum high school GPA and test thresholds, student athletes' academic merit awards must be comparable to those of non-athletes and must be awarded without regard to the student's status as an athlete. Thus a student athlete with a 3.7 GPA and 1400 SAT can't get a more generous academic scholarship than a non-athlete with the same GPA and test score.

The NCAA has strict rules and timelines for athletic recruiting. And athletes need to cast a very wide net in order to find schools that are a fit for them—academically, socially and financially—and whose teams need players like them. Because of the complexity, student athletes benefit tremendously from working with outside resources in recruiting. Those may come from club programs or from independent college consultants who specialize in athletic recruiting, depending on the student and the sport.

If you're the parent of a student athlete, turn the page for a worksheet on athletic priorities.

## WORKSHEET 7: STUDENT ATHLETE PRIORITIES & RESOURCES

To download this worksheet, go to howtopayforcollege.com/htpfc-book-worksheets.

Rank the following in order of priority:

Level of competition ☐     Playing time ☐

College location ☐     Scholarships/total cost ☐

Sports/school/social balance ☐     Teammates/team relationships ☐

Academic environment ☐     Coach ☐

What level am I most interested in playing at? Why?

_____

Separate from the athletic program, what type of college do I want to attend?

_____

My club team's recruiting resources: Will they help me create and promote my athlete profile? Register with the NCAA (if applicable)? Do they have relationships with college coaches? What colleges have other athletes from my club played at?

_____

My high school coach's recruiting resources: Will they help me create and promote my athlete profile? Register with the NCAA (if applicable)? Do they have relationships with college coaches? What colleges have other athletes from my club played at?

_____

Local resources to help with recruiting and college search:

_____

# CHAPTER 8

# Student Loans

## WHAT YOU'LL LEARN IN THIS CHAPTER

Pros and cons of different loan types, what's a reasonable amount to borrow, how to borrow and repay in the federal loan programs.

EARLY IN MY career as a financial advisor, a woman came to me with a typical planning question: She wanted to change career paths to a lower-stress, lower-pay career. The catch was that she was an attorney who still owed several hundred thousand dollars in student loan debt. She had debt from her undergraduate years and from law school in federal and private loans, and had even borrowed from family members. As we sorted through her options, it quickly became apparent that she didn't have many. Although her federal loans were all in income-driven repayment plans with modest monthly payments, she also had large payments on her private loans and had not even begun to make a dent on the money she owed her family. Not only that, but interest was accruing on her federal student loans more rapidly than she was making payments due to how income-driven payment plans work, meaning her loan balances were growing, not shrinking. We calculated that by the end of her 25-year repayment term, she would owe over $300,000 on the federal loans, even though her loan balance when she finished law school was just over $100,000 and she would have paid more than $250,000 toward the loans over the course of her payment plan.

Loan forgiveness is treated as taxable income for those not in Public Service Loan Forgiveness, and at her marginal tax rate that meant she would owe around $125,000 in taxes on the loan forgiveness. And again, she also had private loans and debt to her family. We switched our planning focus from a career change to planning for her eventual insolvency.* I soon realized that there were plenty more people out there like her, so I switched my focus as a financial advisor from helping people plan for retirement to helping people get their kids through college without wrecking their retirement and derailing their kids' aspirations in the process. Because one of the biggest problems with student loan debt is it's too hard to get rid of. It's almost impossible to get student loans discharged in bankruptcy, and yet, despite changes to consumer credit laws making it difficult for young adults to get credit cards, it's incredibly easy for 18-year-olds to commit to student loans that will cast a long shadow over their adult lives.

But for many students, borrowing is what makes going to college possible. Indeed, about two-thirds of the class of 2019 graduated with student loan debt and over 43 million Americans—more than 13% of the U.S. population—have student loans.

It's rare to hear the phrase "student debt" without "crisis" appended. But like most types of debt, there is "good" student debt and "bad" student debt. Good student debt is a reasonable investment in a college education. It results in an affordable payment for a reasonable term post-graduation, one that doesn't cancel out the financial benefits that a college degree confers. Bad student debt curtails opportunities; in

---

\* In IRS terms, "insolvency" is when a taxpayer's debts exceed their assets. Normally, any debt that is forgiven is treated as taxable income. This means that if you have $300,000 in forgiven debt, you owe income taxes on that $300,000. However, if a taxpayer is deemed insolvent, that forgiven debt is not treated as taxable income.

many cases, the individual would have been better off financially had they not attended college.

## How much student loan debt is OK?

So how can you tell the difference *before* you're in over your head? Generally speaking, good borrowing starts—and ends—with the federal student loan programs. To see why, it's instructive to look at who is struggling with student loan payments. The Federal Reserve, in its annual Report on the Economic Well-Being of U.S. Households, reports on the payment status of student loans by borrower segment. Going back to 2019 data (pre-pandemic, and thus not counting the time during the pandemic when federal student loan payments were suspended), the data show that the people struggling with student loan payments are largely not bachelor's degree holders. According to the Fed's survey, only 9% of public university graduates and 7% of private nonprofit college and university graduates are behind on their student loans. Who is behind? Three groups make up the vast majority of struggling borrowers:

- Those who enrolled in college, took out student loans, and then left college without graduating. Of this group, 40% were behind on loan payments.

- Those who attended private for-profit colleges; 24% of graduates of these colleges were behind on payments.

- Those who borrowed for graduate school. Average debt among medical and dental school graduates is over $200,000; for veterinary school graduates it's almost $150,000. Across all disciplines, average debt for graduate students is $82,800. And while some of those career paths—doctors and attorneys, primarily—include compensation packages that make that level of debt a reasonable investment, many careers requiring doctorate-level degrees have salaries in the mid- to high five figures.

Undergraduates who limit borrowing to the federal Direct Student Loan program will graduate owing approximately $28,000; making payments of about $300 per month will have those loans paid off in 10 years. And as we've discussed previously, the earnings increase of a college degree will in most cases cover a $300 monthly loan payment.

## Federal Student Loans

Good news if borrowing is part of your college funding plan: The federal government is happy to lend you money to do so. Federal education loans for the undergraduate years are available through two programs.

### Direct Student Loans

Direct Student Loans are loans taken out by the student and are available to all undergraduates, regardless of credit. The loan amount is capped based on the student's academic year. First-year students can borrow $5,500; second-year students, $6,500; students in their third through fifth years of college can borrow $7,500. Students with financial need may get a portion of their loans "subsidized" meaning that no interest accrues on the loan during the college years and the six-month grace period following graduation. The maximum subsidized amount is $2,000 less than the maximum total amount, so a second-year student's maximum subsidized loan would be $4,500. Independent students—those who are self-supporting rather than supported by their parents—and students whose parents do not qualify for PLUS loans can borrow more—$4,000 more in the first two years and $5,000 more in the remaining years—in unsubsidized loans where interest accrues from the date the loan is disbursed.

Direct Student Loans are also available to graduate students. Graduate students can borrow more than undergraduates—up to $20,500 annually—and are not eligible for interest subsidies.

If you're planning to borrow more than the Direct Student Loan, keep reading.

## Direct PLUS Loans

Direct PLUS Loans are available to parents with good credit. Parents can borrow up to the full cost of attendance minus financial aid and scholarships.

All direct education loans—student loans and PLUS loans—have a set of borrower protections that generally make them the best starting point for borrowing: Fixed interest rates, payment deferral (with interest accruing on non-subsidized loans) during the school years and for a six-month grace period following graduation, income-driven repayment plans, and options to suspend payments during times of financial hardship. If you're still not convinced that federal loans should be your starting point, remember that *only* the federal direct education loans were suspended with no interest accruing during the pandemic.

Interest rates on federal education loans are set in May of each year for loans disbursed on or after July 1 of that year. The interest rate is a set markup from the 10-year Treasury yield, based on loan type:

Direct student loan (undergraduate) = Treasury yield + 2.05%

Direct student loan (graduate) = Treasury yield + 3.6%

Direct PLUS loan (parent) = Treasury yield + 4.6%

Thus for the 2021–2022 school year when the May 10-year Treasury yield was 1.684%, interest rates were:

Direct undergraduate 3.734%

Direct graduate 5.284%

Direct PLUS 6.284%

You can look up rates for the current school year at studentaid.gov.

In addition, federal education loans have origination fees, which are one-time administrative charges levied when the loan is disbursed, or sent to the school to pay college costs. Currently those fees are 1.057% for student loans and 4.228% for PLUS loans. That means that your $5,500 first-year Direct Student Loan will cost $58.14; the same amount in a PLUS loan will cost $232.54.

Discerning readers will note that the Direct Student Loan will always cost less than the PLUS loan. That makes the Direct Student Loan the best starting point for any family's borrowing, regardless of who will ultimately be responsible for the payments.

## Private student loans

While the vast majority of student loan borrowing happens within the federal loan programs, many borrowers opt for private loans instead of or in addition to federal loans. Looking at the interest rates and origination fees on PLUS loans and the low ceiling on Direct Student Loans, it's easy to see why private student loans can be tempting.

Private education loans are offered by many lenders and financial institutions. The terms vary by lender. A few key differentiators between federal and private loans are:

- Private student loans require a co-signer, unlike federal Direct Student Loans, meaning that the co-signer (you) is equally responsible for the loan.

- Interest rates may be variable instead of fixed, and refinancing to lower interest rates later may be offered.

- Repayment options may be quoted for different amounts of time than federal loans, which are quoted on 10- or 25-year repayment schedules.

- Most offer in-school deferment with interest accruing.

- Some lenders may offer limited hardship provisions.

- Private loans cannot be refinanced into federal loans, although federal loans can be refinanced to private.

- Nobody wants to think about ever needing this one, but in the horrific event of the death of the student borrower, new private loans issued after 2018 can be discharged.

Interest paid on any education loan—federal or private, parent or student—up to $2,500 is tax deductible for qualifying taxpayers. The deduction phases out at AGI of $70,000–$85,000 (single/head of household) or $140,000–$170,000 (married filing joint), and is an above-the-line deduction, meaning you can claim it even if you don't itemize. Only the named borrower can take the deduction, regardless of who's making the payments. That means that parents paying off a Direct Student Loan on behalf of the student don't get the interest deduction, but the student would. (Note to parents making these payments on behalf of someone who is eligible for the student loan interest deduction: The deduction is worth about $300, so you might ask them to pick up a payment or two each year.)

## Other types of loans

There are countless other types of loans available, which are discussed below. One important consideration with any loan that is not specifically a student loan is that you will need to begin making payments right away. This can ultimately result in more borrowing, because as you direct your income toward loan payments it's not available for other expenses, which leads to larger loans in subsequent years. Here are some of the most common types of loans families ask about:

### Home equity line of credit (HELOC)

In some cases these can be a reasonable means of borrowing. Interest rates are generally cheaper than for parent PLUS loans and it's possible to make interest-only payments in the initial years of the loan. However:

- HELOCs have variable interest rates so you could end up with a much more expensive loan than anticipated.

- HELOCs typically have a limited withdrawal period—usually 10 years. If you have an existing HELOC, you might not be able to continue withdrawing from it through the college years.

- Interest on the portion of your HELOC used for anything other than a home purchase or renovation is not tax deductible.

 **DANGER:** The collateral for a HELOC is your home. That means if you default on your HELOC, the lender could foreclose on your house.

The case where a HELOC makes sense is usually this one: The parents have some means of paying it off quickly following graduation. This might be the case, for example, when the parents have a specific expectation of money post-graduation, such as a gift or inheritance that they don't want to tap into during the college years.

## 401(k) loans

No, no, NO!! This is a terrible idea:

- Repayment starts immediately and the maximum repayment term is five years.

- If you leave the company, the loan must be fully repaid within 60 days or it will be deemed a distribution, and the balance is added to your taxable income for the year, plus a 10% penalty if you're under age 59 1/2.

## Personal loans

These are a lot like student loans but without the benefits of student loans: Interest isn't deductible and you can't defer payments while in school.

Student loans can be used strategically, too. Let's say that you're eligible for the AOTC. More on that in Chapter 9; the quick summary is that to claim it, your AGI needs to be less than $160,000. If you need to contribute to your 401k in order to bring your AGI below the $160,000 threshold, but doing so will leave you without enough cash to cover college costs, you are probably better off taking out a student loan and contributing to retirement so that you can claim the AOTC, then skipping the retirement contribution in a future year when the AOTC isn't a factor and repaying the loan then. The AOTC is worth up to $2,500 per student per year, which is probably more than the interest that would accrue on the loan before you could repay it.

# Who borrows: Parent or student?

Many parents don't want their students to graduate with student loan debt and prefer to borrow in their own name if borrowing is needed. That's a great sentiment, but don't let it cloud reality. In most cases, it's more beneficial for the student to take out a loan. That's because the fees and interest rates are lower for student loans than for PLUS (parent) loans. Choosing the Direct Student Loan over the parent PLUS loan in your student's first year will accrue about $600 less in interest before the first payment needs to be made. Multiply that by four years—and potentially multiple students in the family—and the savings are considerable.

However, if what you need to borrow exceeds the Direct Student Loan limits ($5,500 for first-year students/$6,500 second year/$7,500 third year and beyond), parents are most likely going to be on the hook for the debt anyway. That's because most private loans require parents to co-sign, and co-signers are equally liable for the debt as are primary borrowers. If that's your situation, then I generally recommend parent PLUS loans in lieu of private loans. The federal protections are great, and you can always choose to refinance into a private loan later when your student graduates and you know what the balance is.

There are a couple of scenarios in which it makes more sense for parents to borrow. The first is when a parent is eligible for Public Service Loan Forgiveness (PSLF) because of public or nonprofit sector employment. In PSLF, the borrower pays a set percentage of their income toward loans for 10 years, after which time the remaining loan balance is forgiven. For a parent borrower to be eligible for PSLF, PLUS loans need to be consolidated into a Direct Consolidation Loan at the start of repayment and then enrolled in an income-driven repayment plan.

The other scenario is when a parent is older and earns a low income. That's because federal loans are non-recourse loans, meaning that if the borrower passes away before the loan is repaid, the balance goes with them. Let's say a parent is 70 when their child enrolls in college, has the median income for someone in their early 70s (about $55,000) and has a life expectancy of about 15 years based on family history. The parent could finance college through PLUS loans, defer the loans throughout the college years, consolidate the loans upon graduation, defer them for another three years, and then enroll in an income-driven repayment plan until their death. If this parent lived 15 years— the average life expectancy of a 70-year-old—they would only make loan payments during half of that time and depending on a few factors might pay as little as $75 per month for that time period, regardless of how much they borrowed.

## How do you actually get a loan?

Loans are easy to take out; repayment can be either very simple or very complex. The first step in taking out loans is to complete the FAFSA.

The FAFSA is the application for Direct Student Loans. Schools may have additional application requirements for parent PLUS loans.

A student may get direct loans—or parent PLUS loans—as part of their financial aid package. If so, then simply accepting the loan component of the aid package will result in you taking out the loan. Otherwise, contact the school's financial aid office to request it. All student borrowers are required to complete loan counseling (an online course) in order to take out a student loan.

Student loans and PLUS loans are disbursed directly to the school and are allocated equally across academic terms. That means that a first-year student on semesters will have $2,750 disbursed per semester; on quarters, $1,833.33 is disbursed per term. The loan is first applied to the student's outstanding bill (tuition, fees, on-campus housing or meal plan, less scholarships and grants); if there's any surplus, the school will forward the remaining amount to the student.

For example, let's say the student lives off campus and takes out a Direct Student Loan for $6,500. Tuition and fees for the semester are $7,000 with a scholarship covering $5,000 of that. The student's balance is $2,000, and a loan for $3,250 (the current semester's half of $6,500) is disbursed. The university will keep $2,000 and give the student the remaining $1,250. If the parents took out a PLUS loan to cover the student's off-campus living costs, that loan would likewise be paid to the school and then forwarded to the student. Families need to plan for this time lag if the first month's rent is due before school starts.

Student loans are automatically deferred while the student is in college and for a six-month grace period following graduation. Non-subsidized loans begin to accrue interest on the day they are disbursed. When the grace period ends and repayment starts, all of the accrued interest is added to the loan principal. So a first-year student who takes out a $5,500 unsubsidized loan with a 3.75% interest rate and never makes a payment will find their loan balance to be around $6,400 when it goes into repayment.

# Repayment options

At the end of the grace period following graduation, loans go into repayment: The monthly payment is calculated and the borrower is notified of the payment amount and when the first payment is due.

Unsubsidized loans accrue interest during that entire period; subsidized loans do not. When the loan goes into repayment, the accrued interest is capitalized, or added to the loan balance. Loan servicers—the companies that manage the loans on behalf of the federal government—automatically enroll borrowers in the Standard repayment plan unless the borrower requests a different one, and then monthly payments begin.

Parent PLUS loans, on the other hand, go into repayment as soon as they're disbursed, although the borrower can choose to defer payments while the student is in school. Note that interest continues to accrue on deferred payments.

The Standard repayment plan is for 10 years. Students who have taken out the full Direct Student Loan every year and not made any payments during school or the grace period will owe between $27,000 and $29,000 total, depending on subsidies and interest rates, and will have fixed monthly payments between $300 and $350 under the Standard plan. This plan generally results in the lowest total borrowing costs because the borrower will pay less interest over the repayment term; however, it also has the highest monthly payment because the loan is fully amortized to be paid off in 10 years. Think of this like a mortgage: A 15-year mortgage will have higher monthly payments than a 30-year mortgage, but over the full repayment term you'll pay less.

Federal student loans have a variety of other payment options that may suit some borrowers better.

Graduated repayment begins with lower monthly payments and increases the payment every two years. Like the Standard plan, these payment plans are also for 10 years. While the lower payments can be beneficial in the early years, the borrower will pay more over the lifetime of the plan due to the higher interest costs.

Borrowers with more than $30,000 in direct or PLUS loan balances can also use the Extended repayment plan, where loans are paid off over 25 years instead of 10.

## Income-driven repayment

Income-driven repayment plans allow borrowers whose loan payments are otherwise unaffordable to make payments based on their discretionary income. There are a variety of income-driven repayment options available, each of which uses a slightly different calculation based on household size, tax filing status and percentage of discretionary income considered available for loan payments. As a general rule, income-driven repayment options make sense when the borrower's loan balance exceeds their annual income, so they come into play most often with PLUS loans for graduate students or parents.

One of the big problems with income-driven repayment plans is that monthly payments are often less than the amount of interest accruing on the loan each month. This results in the borrower's loan balance growing over time, despite continuous monthly payments (think of the attorney at the beginning of this chapter). Another client of mine borrowed $70,000 to attend graduate school. After 10 years in an income-driven repayment plan, she had paid $80,000 on her loans and her balance had increased to $85,000. Borrowers in income-driven plans are eligible for loan forgiveness after 20 or 25 years of payments, but currently that loan forgiveness is taxable. That means that the forgiven loan balance is added to the borrower's income in the year it's forgiven and they pay taxes on that balance. If my client were to continue in her income-driven plan for another

15 years, based on her current path, she would pay about $120,000 more in loan payments and owe around $110,000. Between payments and taxes on the forgiveness, her $70,000 student loan balance would cost her about $235,000. Awful, right? And that's the situation I'd like you to avoid.

## Public Service Loan Forgiveness

PSLF isn't a payment plan but an option for borrowers who work in the public or nonprofit sectors. Under PSLF, a borrower enters an income-driven repayment plan and if they continue working in the public or nonprofit sector and making loan payments in an income-driven plan, they can apply for forgiveness of the remaining loan balance after 10 years. Besides limiting the repayment period to 10 years, PSLF loan forgiveness is nontaxable. Were my client eligible, then her $70,000 loan balance would have only cost her a total of $80,000 in payments because of the shorter repayment period and nontaxable forgiveness. Much more manageable, but unfortunately these plans have extraordinarily complex rules that make it very difficult to qualify for forgiveness. Many PSLF borrowers had their loans forgiven under the Temporary Waiver program in place through October 2022. As of this writing, it remains to be seen whether the forgiveness process will be simplified for all PSLF borrowers going forward.

Parent PLUS loans can be enrolled in PSLF if they're first consolidated into a Direct Consolidation Loan. A parent employed by an eligible institution (public sector or nonprofit) who will remain in that role for at least 10 years following the student's graduation might consider using PLUS loans to finance college and then enrolling in PSLF.

One important point about loans in deferment (during school or the grace period) or income-driven repayment plans is that any payments made are credited to accrued interest first. That's why borrowers in income-driven plans see their balances grow over time: If you owe

$50,000 with a 5% interest rate, your loans accrue $7 in interest every day. If your monthly payment is only $50 and you're accruing $210 (30 x $7) in interest every month, then every month your balance grows by $160. After a year, you'll have almost $2,000 in accrued interest and until you've paid that off, you won't make any headway on your loan principal. If you continue making income-based payments for several years, that accrued interest number can quickly become insurmountable.

## Should you make loan payments during the school years?

No payments are required on student loans until six months after graduation. PLUS loans can also be deferred during school. However, except in the case of Direct subsidized loans, interest accrues on the loans. Which begs the question, should you make payments on your loan(s) while in school? The answer depends on the interest rate.

Let's say your student is taking out the Direct Student Loan every year and they have an extra $2,000 from a summer job after the second year that they could use to pay down your balances or pay for this year's costs. Their first-year loan has an interest rate of 2.75%, the second-year loan is at 3.734%, and the interest rate for the coming year is 4.1%. In that case, they're better off putting money toward this year's costs and reducing the amount they'll borrow for the current year since the interest rate is higher.

With PLUS loans the calculus is similar, although with PLUS loans the choice is whether to defer, not whether to proactively make payments. PLUS loan holders might choose to only make payments on their highest interest loan(s) during the school years to minimize interest accrual. With PLUS loans, parents can also "refinance" prior years' higher interest loans by taking out larger loans in lower interest years and using the excess to pay off a prior year's higher rate loan. For

137

example, if PLUS loan interest rates were 7.4% in the first year and 5.8% in the second year, a parent who was planning to borrow $5,000 per year might take out $10,000 in the second year and use half of it to pay off the first year's loan balance.

It's always a good idea to make payments during the grace period, if at all possible. That's because accrued interest capitalizes—it's added to the loan balance and then begins accruing its own interest—when the loan goes into repayment, so payments made during the grace period result in dollar-for-dollar reductions in the loan balance, and not making any payments means you'll spend 10 years paying interest on your interest. Again, target the loans with the highest interest rates when making payments during the grace period.

Let's say a student could put $2,000 toward loans during the grace period, and their interest rates range from 2.75% to 5.045%. Paying down the higher rate loan instead of the lower rate loan would save $262 more over the course of repayment.

## Paying off loans more quickly

Even though interest rates and payments on Direct Student Loans are generally pretty reasonable, paying them off sooner rather than later is often beneficial. One big reason to pay them off quickly: If your student goes to graduate school, loans are automatically put in deferment while they are enrolled in a graduate program. With interest accruing for several years, loan balances can balloon.

There are two primary means of paying down debt: The "snowball" or the "avalanche." In both approaches, you make the minimum payment on all of your loans except one. In the avalanche approach, you make extra payments on your highest interest rate loan first. Once it's paid off, you direct your surplus toward your next highest interest rate loan, and so on until the debt is fully repaid. In the snowball approach, your extra payments go toward your smallest loan balance.

Once it's repaid, you target the next smallest, and so on, reducing the total number of loans on which you owe money.

The avalanche will save the most money over time. However, with student loans the snowball can often be most beneficial, at least as a starting point. That's because many borrowers struggle to find any extra cash for student loans, especially in the early years of repayment, so paying off a single loan is often the best way to free up extra cash to make larger payments on other loans. It's really a function of how much extra you can pay each month. If it's not a lot, then pay off a small loan quickly because you can add that loan's payment to the amount you can target elsewhere.

## Loan consolidation

Federal loans cannot be refinanced, but they can be consolidated so that multiple loans become a single loan with a single payment. Consolidation may seem like a great idea, but it usually isn't. Your loans' interest rates are averaged and then rounded up to the nearest one-eighth of a percent, so you'll pay more interest. In addition, since you now have a single loan at a blended interest rate, you can't target extra payments toward higher interest rate loans.

Loan consolidation can make sense in a few circumstances. A parent PLUS loan borrower who is eligible for PSLF will need to consolidate their PLUS loans into a Direct Consolidation Loan to enroll in PSLF. Consolidation can also make a borrower eligible for an extended repayment term. Otherwise, borrowers can manage payments on multiple loans more effectively by simply enrolling in automatic payment.

# Federal loan hardship provisions

At any point in the repayment process, a borrower with federal loans can access hardship provisions to temporarily reduce or even eliminate monthly payments. The primary means of reducing or eliminating payments are deferment, forbearance, or entering an income-driven repayment plan. Deferment and forbearance suspend all payments for a certain time period; however, interest continues to accrue except on subsidized loans in deferment. Most loan servicers will point borrowers with hardships toward deferment or forbearance; however, most borrowers are better served by enrolling in an income-driven repayment plan. There are numerous reasons for that, the primary one being that payments under income-driven repayment count towards loan forgiveness and may be calculated to be as low as $0 monthly. Yep, $0.

Everything about repayment here is specific to the federal student loan programs. Private lenders have their own terms and programs. If, despite my protesting, you are considering private loans, whether for initial borrowing or to refinance existing loans, your own due diligence is required to learn about the loan terms including any provisions for hardships.

A good borrowing plan looks like this: Use the Direct Student Loan first. If you need additional borrowing at some point during the college years, such as when you have multiple kids in college, use PLUS loans next, but limit borrowing to an amount you can repay within three to five years of graduation—or sooner if your goal is to retire less than three to five years after graduation. If your college plan shows that you need to borrow more than that, you need to expand your college search list.

Now turn the page for a worksheet on borrowing.

# WORKSHEET 8: STUDENT LOANS

To download this worksheet, go to howtopayforcollege.com/htpfc-book-worksheets.

Estimated annual borrowing need: $ _____

Is this more than $6,750 (the average annual Direct Student Loan amount)?

Yes ❏    No ❏

Multiply annual borrowing need by 4 for total amount borrowed: $ _____

Look up current interest rates:

Direct student loan (studentaid.gov/understand-aid/types/ loans/interest rates): _____ %

Parent PLUS loan: _____ %

Private student loan (look up rates from your bank, credible.com, nerdwallet.com): _____ %

Use Bankrate.com to calculate monthly payment for 10-year repayment:

Monthly payment: $ _____

Total amount paid: $ _____

Total interest paid: $ _____

Look up average monthly salary for a 25-year-old in a career path your student might pursue: $ _____

Divide loan payment by monthly salary to determine percent of your income that would go to debt repayment: $ _____

# CHAPTER 9

# Other Sources of Money

## WHAT YOU'LL LEARN IN THIS CHAPTER

Where to find additional dollars that can bring the cost of college in line with your budget, whether from the college, the federal government, or elsewhere.

ALEX WAS ACCEPTED to two colleges. His top choice was more expensive than his second choice, so we tasked him with figuring out how to close the gap. He went to visit the school and was introduced to several current students who turned out to be a goldmine of knowledge on saving money. He learned that by working in the dining halls he could get a discount on his meals. The school had a hard time recruiting enough male resident assistants, so most who applied were hired. And by the way, his top choice school guaranteed tuition and fees for four years, meaning our tuition costs wouldn't go up at all as long as he graduated on time, compared with the 8% average annual tuition inflation rate. All by way of saying, there are plenty of additional sources of money out there that can shave thousands of dollars off your college costs.

# Tax credits

The federal government is your first stop for free money for college. That free money comes from tax credits for education. If you're eligible for the AOTC, you can save $10,000 per student over four years by claiming it every year.

The AOTC is worth up to $2,500 per year, per student, based on qualified higher education expenses (QHEEs) incurred in a calendar year. Specifically, it's calculated as 100% of the first $2,000 of QHEEs and 25% of the next $2,000 of QHEEs. That means that spending $4,000 on QHEEs will reduce your federal income tax bill by $2,500. For AOTC purposes, QHEEs are tuition, fees, books and supplies— not room and board.

Like many tax benefits, the AOTC has an income phaseout. Nonetheless, about 85% of households are eligible for the AOTC. The AOTC phases out for single (or head of household) filers at incomes between $80,000 and $90,000; married filing jointly phases out between $160,000 and $180,000.

The AOTC is a great example of the different ways income can be a factor in college planning, and why planning is key in getting the money you're entitled to. Since it's a tax credit offered by the IRS, the AOTC is based simply on AGI. That means that your pre-tax retirement contributions, or contributions to an FSA or HSA, will reduce your income and can be used to make you eligible for the AOTC. For example, in a two-parent household with total income of $185,000, a contribution of $25,000 to a 401k or HSA would result in AGI of $160,000 and full eligibility for the AOTC. Families who don't max out their retirement or HSA contributions could bunch those savings contributions into years in which they're eligible for the AOTC in order to maximize the benefit. For example, if the above family normally only contributed $15,000 annually to retirement, they could increase those contributions to $25,000 during college years in order to claim the AOTC, then reduce the contributions when the AOTC is no longer a factor.

"But wait!" you're saying. "I just reduced my pre-tax retirement contributions because Roth contributions are better on the FAFSA. If I now need to increase pre-tax contributions to qualify for the AOTC, how do I decide which is more important?"

Good question!

First, check if you are actually receiving need-based financial aid. Despite the best possible FAFSA planning, it's entirely possible you are not receiving need-based scholarships. If that's the case, then your income no longer matters for FAFSA purposes.

If you *are* receiving need-based aid, look at the income years that count. FAFSA income is prior-prior year, meaning that the last income year that matters for the FAFSA is the year that runs through December 31 of your student's sophomore year of college. You have five potential years to claim the AOTC, since four academic years span five calendar (tax) years. It's possible that only one income year will matter for both the FAFSA and the AOTC. Of course, families with multiple college students will have more overlapping years; again, the relative importance of FAFSA and financial aid vs tax credit eligibility can help guide decisions. The worksheet at the end of this chapter lets you calculate the adjustments you'd need to make to become eligible for the AOTC, which you can compare with your financial aid strategies in the previous worksheet.

The quick summary is, *if every student in your household attends a college that meets 100% of financial need through grants* then it's pretty close to a wash whether you go for the AOTC or the FAFSA reduction. Otherwise, you're better off claiming the AOTC even if that means a slight decrease in need-based financial aid—but wait to claim the AOTC until the tax year that begins January of your student's first year of college, and claim it in the four calendar years that run through their college graduation year.

Here's a quick calculation: If you're in the 22% tax bracket (which you are if you're in the AOTC phaseout range), then your pre-tax retirement contributions cost you 10.3 cents in EFC increase per dollar of contribution (22% tax reduction on income x 47% income assessment rate). If you need to contribute $10,000 more to retirement to reduce AGI from $170,000 to $160,000 and get the full AOTC, then that $10,000 saved you $1,250 in taxes (because of the phaseout, you would have received 50% of the value of the AOTC) or 12.5%, whereas it cost you $1,034 in increased EFC. The tax savings from that $10,000 contribution would increase your EFC by $1,034. In that case, the AOTC is worth $216 more.

"But wait!" you're still saying. "How can I pay for college if I'm contributing all this money to retirement?" This is one place where strategic borrowing can make sense. At current interest rates—3.73% for the Direct Student Loan and 6.24% for the parent PLUS loan—a family that borrowed in their student's first year to make up for cash flow constraints from contributing $10,000 to retirement (an after-tax income reduction of $7,800 based on federal taxes only) would accrue about $880 in interest on those loans by college graduation. Depending on interest rates and loan types, it might be cheaper to borrow during the college years if additional retirement contributions are needed to bring the family's AGI below the threshold to claim the AOTC, and then repay those loans later when retirement contributions are reduced.

Divorced parents also have a planning opportunity with the AOTC. Only the parent who claims the student on their tax return can claim the AOTC. If one parent is eligible for the AOTC based on income and the other is not, the eligible parent should claim the student on their tax return. With the dependent tax credit being only $500 for children over age 17, the AOTC is far more valuable. Divorced parents who can cooperate on this can get an extra $10,000 per student over four years. Claiming the student on your tax return is a separate consideration from who is the custodial parent on the FAFSA, so that need not influence your AOTC planning.

Just remember how tax credits like the AOTC work: They reduce your tax bill. They are not mailed out to you (or to your college). That means that if you change your withholding or simply wait for a refund, you need to identify those dollars as part of your college budget if you want them to be available for college.

Families who are eligible for the AOTC should be aware of a few nuances in claiming it:

- Qualified expenses for the AOTC are more limited than for 529s: Only tuition, required fees, books and required supplies are eligible; room and board are not.

- You have to actually pay the expense in the calendar year in which you're claiming it, regardless of what academic period the expense is for. That means that if your spring tuition for 2023 is due by December 31, 2022, you won't be able to claim the AOTC in 2023 for that tuition payment. However, if the college offers a payment plan for some of the tuition and you make payments in 2023, the portion paid in 2023 is eligible for the AOTC, which might justify paying a finance charge for a payment plan. This is different from your 529, where you can take a distribution in December to pay January's tuition bill.

- In order to claim the AOTC you cannot have paid the qualified expenses with a distribution from your 529 plan. That means that if you're eligible for the AOTC, you need to spend $4,000 either out of pocket or by taking out loans in order to claim it. If you have enough for the full cost of college in your 529 and are eligible for the AOTC, you might consider having the student take out $2,000 in Direct Student Loans each year to get the AOTC, then use your 529 to pay off the loan.

- The AOTC is not indexed for inflation. That means that families who are close to the income limit at the start of college may exceed it in later years. Increasing pre-tax retirement contributions can help get under the threshold, but it may take some planning to remain eligible for all four years.

The final important point about the AOTC is that it's not automatic. You need to file IRS Form 8863 with your tax return to claim it.

The AOTC is one of two tax credits that can help pay the bills. The other is the Lifetime Learning Credit, but the AOTC is usually more beneficial for families of undergraduate students, and you can only claim one tax credit per year. The AOTC gets you a $2,500 tax credit for $4,000 of expenses, whereas the LLC is a 20% tax credit for up to $10,000 of QHEEs, meaning the maximum annual tax credit is $2,000. Furthermore, eligibility for the LLC phases out at lower incomes: $59,000 for single filers and $118,000 for married filing jointly. The LLC does have two advantages over the AOTC, though: You can claim it for more than four years, and you can claim it for graduate school, professional school, or courses taken "to get or improve job skills."[1]

# Free money from your school

Your next big source of free money is your student's college. When you're in the college research and application stage, this can result in needing to do a lot of research. Here are some examples of on-campus opportunities that can go a long way toward filling the gap between cost and budget.

## Resident assistants

RAs are students with supervisory positions within dorms. Depending on the college, duties can include community-building, assisting students with personal needs, conflict or crisis management, operations and administration of residence halls, and even disciplinary or security responsibilities such as verifying IDs of individuals entering dorms. During the 2020–2021 school year, for example, many RAs were responsible for enforcing pandemic policies within their dorms. Compensation varies depending on the responsibilities, but typically RAs get free or discounted room and board in lieu of cash compensation.

Being an RA is a significant commitment, usually requiring considerably more hours and engagement than a typical student job since the RA lives in the dorm with students. Some colleges have similar roles with lesser commitments and lesser compensation. For example, my daughter's college has a dorm-based role organizing weekly house meetings that has a small stipend attached to it.

## Departmental scholarships

Many departments within colleges offer their own scholarships to students pursuing those majors, and not just for niche majors. Yes, our friend whose son is studying meteorology was offered scholarships by the meteorology department of each college he applied to, but plenty of business and even humanities departments have scholarships available; other scholarships are offered to students pursuing specific careers such as teaching. Some of these scholarships are listed on the school's financial aid website, but often you have to reach out directly to the department to learn more. In many cases, departmental scholarships are only available to students after they declare a major, so first-year students might not be eligible now but could be later on.

## Research projects

Just because you're looking at liberal arts colleges, don't assume no research happens there. Research isn't just in labs; plenty goes on in social sciences and humanities, too. Generally, schools have funds available to compensate student researchers or can leverage work-study for eligible students. As an added benefit, sometimes research can be combined with a classroom project so that the student gets academic credit for their research too. The range and availability of research opportunities varies tremendously from school to school and even department to department, as does compensation since it's often grant-funded, so again this is something to investigate at each school you are considering. It's fairly common for research grants to be $1,000 per academic term or more, so don't overlook research as a tool for closing the gap.

## Jobs with perks

Of course students can get jobs and earn money. Here's the thing: A lot of jobs—on-campus and off—have added benefits you should look for. Most food service jobs offer free or discounted meals; on-campus food services jobs sometimes even discount the student's entire meal plan. Bookstore employees may get discounts on books. Just remember to look for a job with perks that save money you have to spend; as a former retail worker and a parent of retail workers, I can guarantee you that working in a clothing store will not save you money even though you do "need" clothes.

## Tuition freezes or guarantees

Some colleges freeze tuition and fees for four years, meaning that no matter how much tuition increases for new students, those already enrolled will pay the same tuition all four years. With tuition inflation averaging 8% annually, keeping your tuition payment flat for four years can mean thousands of dollars in savings. Freshman year's $20,000 in tuition would increase by $1,600 in one year and total over $25,000 for senior year at 8% annual inflation. Guaranteed tuition for all four years is almost like a secret scholarship.

## What about internships?

Good news: Most summer internships for college students are paid, and many of them pay quite well. In fact, the average hourly pay for interns in the summer of 2020 was over $20.[2] And about 75% of college graduates participate in a summer internship at least once during their college career. Even better: Most high-paying internships aren't available until at least the summer after the student's second year of college, meaning these earnings don't impact their FAFSA.

Colleges provide varying levels of support for internship-seeking students, and often that support varies by major. Pre-professional majors such as business and engineering tend to track students into internships, at least for the summer before senior year. Programs within a college often have relationships with employers which can simplify the internship hiring process. And Handshake and other online tools mean that students are not limited by their school's location in finding internships. Alex, for example, landed an internship at a Fortune 500 company across the country, via Handshake.

With all that good news about internships, about 40% of internships remain unpaid, especially those in government or the nonprofit sector. (The Fair Labor Standards Act has very strict rules about for-profit entities hiring unpaid interns.) Some colleges provide stipends or grants to support students in unpaid internships; students considering working in the public sector where most internships are unpaid would be wise to learn about such stipends at their top choice colleges.

# Other people's money

What about if someone just says they want to help pay for your student's college? If you are so fortunate as to have people like that in your life, there are a few good options:

## Contributing to your *existing* 529

Most 529 plans have gifting pages. If your benefactor is a resident of your state and your state offers a tax benefit for contributions, you both win if they gift to your 529.

## Setting up their own 529

This is a good strategy for larger gifts, especially with the FAFSA eliminating the "Money paid on your behalf" question which previously required students to report distributions from 529s owned by anyone other than their parent as student income. This allows the donor to retain some level of control over the gift and keeps it off your student's FAFSA.

## Cash gifts

Your student is best served if cash gifts are given to you, the parent, who can then hand them over to the student. Grandparents who want to pay tuition directly to avoid federal gift limits should only do so if the student is not receiving need-based financial aid, or if they're willing to give enough to offset the aid the student will lose. Tuition payments made by a third party are treated in the financial aid formula the same way as outside scholarships: They reduce need-based aid by 50 cents on the dollar.

Here's the important thing about gifts: If anyone tells you they would like to help with college, you need to ask them for specifics. The most financially savvy way to give $500 is different from the right way to give $5,000 or $50,000. Not only that, but if these gifts are large enough to close the affordability gap at some of the schools your student is interested in, you want to know about that when your student is deciding whether or not to apply or to accept.

And of course, ask the gifter to wait until after you've filed the FAFSA to hand over the cash!

## Tuition reimbursement programs

Many employers—including the ones that students tend to work for, such as Chipotle and Starbucks—offer tuition reimbursement for employees. Students are required to work a minimum number of hours weekly for a set timeframe—usually a minimum of six months, but often more—in order to become eligible; upon eligibility, the employer reimburses a portion of tuition. These programs essentially work as scholarships: You work a certain amount, and the employer gives you some money for college.

Some employers offer similar benefits for parents of college students, so check your benefits package to see if you are eligible for any tuition benefits or if your employer offers scholarships for employee's children. Unfortunately for the self-employed, you cannot set up a tuition reimbursement program for the benefit of the employer's children.

Now turn the page for a worksheet on getting more money.

## WORKSHEET 9: OTHER SOURCES OF MONEY

To download this worksheet, go to howtopayforcollege.com/htpfc-book-worksheets.

# AOTC eligibility

Look up your adjusted gross income (AGI) from last year's tax
return (line 11):                                                          $ _____

- Is it less than $160,000 (married) or $80,000 (single)? If so, you are eligible.
  Otherwise, consider the following:

## Eligibility strategies

- Increase pre-tax retirement contributions (check pay stub to see if you are
  maximizing or how much more you could contribute).
- Increase HSA contributions.

# Money from the College

- On-campus jobs with outside benefits available:

  _____

  _____

# Other Money

- Does your employer offer tuition reimbursement or scholarships for
  employees' children?
- Requirements & amount:

  _____

  _____

- Does your student's employer offer tuition reimbursement or scholarships
  for employees?
- Requirements & amount:

  _____

  _____

- Who has said they'll help? What amounts can you confirm:

  _____

  _____

# CHAPTER 10

# Your College Budget

## WHAT YOU'LL LEARN IN THIS CHAPTER

How to create a budget for college.

G ABI AND ALEX are twins, yet are very different students who had very different college goals. As a result, they had different college budgets, despite having similar savings and the ability of their parents (Bob and me) to pay out of pocket being the same. Alex wanted a big college experience with football Saturdays and big social events. However, his high school experience—with most of his effort going to extracurriculars and sports—left us uninterested in doing a lot of financial heavy lifting for college. His budget was the cost of in-state public school. Gabi, on the other hand, was a personality better suited to smaller colleges. Not only that, but she had worked her tail off through high school and excelled in a demanding academic environment. We wanted her to have the option of private colleges, but that didn't mean unlimited options. It meant that depending on scholarships and financial aid, she might need to have some skin in the game. Each had a different college budget, even though we could have chosen to pay an equal amount for both. I think it's possible to be fair without being completely equal. They may or may not agree with me, but I don't think either of them wants to attend the other's college, so I'm probably right about this.

Now that you know all the places money can come from, it's time to develop a draft college budget. We'll create a detailed spending plan later, but your student will have a much easier time finding affordable colleges if they know what your family can afford.

Good news: Since most people hate budgeting at least as much as they hate dieting, this will be the shortest chapter in this book. Bad news: If you hate budgeting, it might be the most important.

To figure out your annual college budget, add the numbers for:

1/4 of your college savings

+

The amount you can pay annually from your income

+

The amount your student can pay annually from their income

+

Any annual amount someone else is gifting to help
pay for college

+

1/4 of any savings anyone else has set aside for your
student's education

+

If you are eligible for the AOTC, add $2,500

+

If you are willing to have your student take out loans, add
$6,750, as the average annual borrowing amount

= Your College Budget

For example, if you have $50,000 in savings, can pay $8,000 per year from your income and $2,000 from your student's, have $4,000 per year coming from grandma and are eligible for the AOTC, your budget looks like this:

$12,500 from savings ($50,000 / 4)

$8,000 from parents

$2,000 from student

$4,000 from grandparents

$2,500 from AOTC

=$29,000

If your family is willing to borrow, increase that by $6,750 for an annual budget of $35,750.

If you want a bigger budget, now is a great time to brainstorm with your student how you might get there. Your student may be able to find some additional scholarships. They may be able to get higher-paying summer jobs. You may be able to save more.

Families who really need to stretch their budget should look for opportunities to reduce the number of years spent in college. If your student is taking AP or IB classes or enrolled in an early college program, they might be able to graduate in less than four years. Starting at a community college might be a good pathway. Your state may offer a dual-enrollment program that allows students to complete their first two years of college at a community college adjacent to a four-year college, while still living on campus and experiencing student life.

Here's some good news: Whatever your budget, you will find good choices. And even if those choices aren't what you intended, they will leave your student in a better place than they would be in by borrowing more.

Here's more good news: In the next few chapters, you'll learn how to look for colleges that are likely to meet your budget.

Now turn the page, take a deep breath, and let's map out your budget.

## WORKSHEET 10: COLLEGE BUDGET

To download this worksheet, go to howtopayforcollege.com/htpfc-book-worksheets. The online worksheet will calculate values for different numbers of years in college.

# Our Non-Loan Resources For Paying For College

### Our College Savings

| | |
|---|---|
| Our College Savings | $ _____ |
| Other People's College Savings | $ _____ |
| Additional Amounts We Can Save | $ _____ |
| One-time Outside Scholarships | $ _____ |
| **College Savings Total** | $ _____ |
| **Divide by 4 for Annual Contribution from Savings** | $ _____ |

### Our Contributions from Income

| | |
|---|---|
| Annual Income from Parents | $ _____ |
| Annual Income from Student* | $ _____ |
| Annual Contribution from Others | $ _____ |
| **Annual Income Total** | $ _____ |

### Outside Scholarships

| | |
|---|---|
| Annual Outside Scholarships | $ _____ |
| **Outside Scholarships Total** | $ _____ |

### American Opportunity Tax Credit

| | |
|---|---|
| Annual Credit of $2,500 (if eligible) | $ _____ |
| **Tax Credit Total** | $ _____ |

# Our Annual College Budget

| | |
|---|---|
| Annual Contribution from Savings | $ _____ |
| Annual Contribution from Income | $ _____ |
| Total Outside Scholarship | $ _____ |
| AOTC | $ _____ |
| **Annual College Budget** | $ _____ |

# CHAPTER 11

# Researching Colleges

How to find out what you really need to know about a college, the best search tools out there to help you, and what questions you should be asking along the way.

ONCE A STUDENT takes the PSAT, they get bombarded with college emails. Emails full of happy, attractive, diverse groups of young adults frolicking—often books in hand—in ivy-covered quads, studying in ornate libraries, cheering their team to victory, peering intently through microscopes... All of the colleges are fabulous, at least as seen through this lens, and a lot of them are really good at marketing to teens. Gabi was interested in all of them. Literally. She replied to so many colleges who offered more content or freebies that she had to get a new email address. She was most interested in out-of-state colleges, so we planned an "East Coast-plus" college tour during the summer between junior and senior years of high school. Unfortunately, I didn't have two months off work and an unlimited travel budget to visit all the schools she "loved," so we needed to cull the list somehow.

Since I'm me, cost was at the top of my list of decision criteria, but Gabi had some additional priorities. In high school, she pursued two passions: theater and computer science. Her biggest fear about going to college was that she would have to choose one or the other, so she wanted a college that allowed her to pursue both, and not just in the classroom. She also required her college to be bigger than her high school (about 2,000 students). She loved going out in Portland, whether to the theater or sports events or restaurants or just hanging out downtown, so she wanted an urban setting. Not only that, but—like most 16-year-olds—she had some priorities that I—like most parents—didn't think were the best ones. So while we were on the one hand trying to shrink her list—or at least our trip—to something manageable, I was also trying to add some schools that she wasn't interested in. (Spoiler alert: Those ended up being her top choice schools. So don't feel guilty about doing this yourself.) Those criteria allowed us to shorten our college tour to one week, including some family visits, and we got to see 20 different colleges—which was still quite a lot more than she would be able to apply to.

Whether you plan to tour colleges in person or not, you need some tools for both finding the right schools to apply to and narrowing down your list. You might not love figuring this stuff out—and that's why you're getting a step-by-step process.

## Researching in-state

Your starting point for research should be your in-state public schools. Cost being one of the key considerations here, this will give you a baseline estimate for what four years of college will cost your family. Your in-state cost has a few components:

- The total cost of attendance at the college(s) you're interested in. This should include not just published cost, but what's included in that cost. For example, many colleges—especially public ones—have different price tiers for housing and meal plans, and they get to choose which go into the Cost of Attendance.

- Any merit awards you'll be eligible for, including selection criteria. Do you need to apply, or are you considered automatically? Many colleges have both automatically-awarded scholarships and others requiring applications. Do they use weighted or unweighted GPA? What about test scores?

- Pathways available in your state such as free community college or dual enrollment, where a student enrolls in both a community college and a four-year college and attends the community college for their first two years while living on campus and having access to other aspects of student life at the four-year college.

You should consider some other items with your in-state school, which will vary by student. For example, is there an honors college? What about student engagement through things like academic residential communities, intramural sports, and other activities that can help students find a home on a big campus?

Most students also have access to regional tuition exchanges, which allow students to attend neighboring states' public colleges at in-state or slightly above in-state tuition rates. Examples include the Western Undergraduate Exchange, the Academic Common Market, the Midwest Student Exchange, and the New England Regional Student Program. Each program, and each school participating in one of these programs, has an application process and criteria. You can find current rules by Googling any of the above names.

## Find your fabulous

When every college looks fabulous on paper (or online as the case may be), how do you decide which fabulous is *your* fabulous? When it comes to cost, the following section outlines some of the major considerations. You'll also find some pointers about non-financial factors that might help your student find schools that are good academic and social fits. Because after all, finding your fit the first time around and graduating without transferring is the best money-saving strategy.

## Financial aid policies

It's not enough to have a low SAI. What a school does with your SAI is far more important than the number itself. Do they meet financial need? If so, do they meet full need or just partial? Do they meet the need through grants or are loans and work-study part of the package? And which financial aid form do they use, the FAFSA or CSS Profile? Most families will have a lower SAI on the FAFSA than on the Profile, so a school that meets full need based on the FAFSA will usually cost less than one that meets full need based on the Profile.

## Merit scholarship availability

Many, but by no means all, schools offer merit scholarships. As we discussed previously, merit scholarships are used by schools to build the student body they want. Schools like the Ivy Leagues enroll plenty of phenomenal students, so they don't need to offer scholarships to attract more good students. The majority of merit scholarships are based on academics—grades and sometimes test scores—because colleges want to attract high-performing students. So if a student is in the top quartile academically at a school that offers merit, they're probably going to get some scholarships. But putting together a student body is a lot like putting together a football team: You can't fill up a whole team with wide receivers and running backs; you also need a center and a punter. What that means is, there may be other things that a school is looking for that can lead to scholarships. For example, small colleges love to be able to say they have students from all 50 states. That means you might increase your chances of getting a scholarship to small private colleges if you look out of state, especially if you're from a small state.

## Transfer credit policy

Newsflash: Not all colleges grant credit for advanced classes taken in high school. If your student took a full load of AP or IB classes with the intent of getting college credit and graduating in less than four years, that needs to be one of your search criteria. Colleges may offer one or more of the following, dependent on the student's exam results:

- Credit toward the student's major.

- General education (elective) credit.

- Advanced standing (accelerating graduation by one or more academic terms).

- Placement without credit, where the student skips some entry level classes but doesn't receive any credit.

Schools set their own minimum score requirements to actually get credit, so in many cases you may not know for sure until well after you've made your college selection. It's not unusual for schools to either cap the total number of credits a student can use toward their college degree, cap the credits toward a major, require a minimum number of advanced courses to get any placement, or not count any credit earned as a high school student. For example, Gabi's college allows a maximum of three college courses to be fulfilled outside the college itself and requires their own placement exams for many subjects.

# Online research

There are a ton of great tools online to help—and also some terrible ones. Below are a few of my favorites, including some tips on using them and where to find the data to fill out this chapter's worksheet.

## Collegedata

Collegedata has probably the best combination of information and ease of use of the big college search sites. It uses the Common Data Set, which is a collaborative effort between colleges and publishers such as *U.S. News & World Report* and the College Board to improve the quality of data available to students and families. Participation in the Common Data Set is optional, so not all colleges are included; however, it's required for consideration in *U.S. News'* college rankings, so most participate. Within Collegedata, you can create an account, enter your student's information, and ask the system to identify schools that are a fit. Or you can research schools individually. To find the above information, you'll use the following tabs for schools you're interested in:

- The **Overview** page shows admission rate, average GPAs and test scores, cost of attendance, average need met, academic calendar, class size and four-year graduation rate. That last statistic is a good one: The Department of Education tracks six-year graduation rate, not four-year. Families wanting to pay for only four years of college would be wise to check four-year graduation rates! Averages for things like GPAs and financial aid are helpful mostly in determining whether you want to take a deeper look.

- **Financials** is the page where you'll get the details about costs and a link to the school's net price calculator. You'll find not just cost of attendance, but also what kinds of financial aid are offered and to whom, and what financial aid form the college requires—FAFSA or CSS Profile. The Financials tab shows how many students applied for aid, how many were determined to have need, how many had full need met and the average percent of need met. It also shows who gets merit aid and the average merit award. Finally, the Financials tab lists other scholarships available to students.

- **Admissions** shows the academic profile of admitted students. There's a lot of helpful information about the admissions process, such as application deadline and essay and other requirements. The most helpful thing at this point is to scroll down to the GPA and test scores section. This shows you a breakdown of the student body by GPA ranges and middle 50% test scores. This is a great tool for determining your likelihood of getting merit awards: If you're in the top 25% academically among students at a college that offers merit, you'll probably get some merit scholarships. Similarly, if your test scores are above the middle 50% range, then you should submit them, even if the college is test-optional.

- **Academics** has information on transfer credit policies, though often it's more directional than definitive: You can see that credit or standing is offered, but you might need to visit the school's website for details.

One key point about Collegedata and the Common Data Set: It's a voluntary, non-audited system that is used in part to compile college rankings. So while there is a great deal of fantastic information here, it's worth double-checking any data points that have particular bearing on your likelihood to apply or attend with specifics on the school's own website.

## College Navigator

College Navigator uses the IPEDS database, which is a compulsory data set collected by the U.S. Department of Education. There are a lot of commonalities between Collegedata and College Navigator, with both sites showing academic and financial information and allowing students to create a profile and let the site suggest fits, but College Navigator has a few elements that are really helpful and make up for its less user-friendly interface:

- The **Net Price** tab shows average net price and average net price by income. It also links directly to the school's net price calculator.

- The **Financial Aid** tab details the components of the school's financial aid packages including federal, state, and institutional grants and federal and other student loans.

- The **General Information** tab shows whether classes are taught by graduate student TAs, listing how many graduate students are in instructional positions.

- **Campus Security** shows crimes and disciplinary actions, for the campus as a whole and within student housing.

## Big Future

Big Future is the College Board's website and offers a similar suite of data on admissions, financial aid and scholarships. One tool Big Future offers, under the **Academics & GPA** tab, is "How do I stack up?" This allows the student to input their GPA, coursework information, test scores and class rank, and see where they fall relative to the student body. In addition, the **Paying** tab shows payment plans offered.

For those looking to expand their search list, Big Future also shows other schools that people looking at a specific school also viewed, to give you an idea of some similar options.

## College Scorecard

This site, run by the U.S. Department of Education, looks at colleges through a different lens: Outcomes. It shows graduation rates, salary ranges for graduates, and average salary by major. In addition, it shows average federal student loan debt and monthly loan payments for both student loans and parent PLUS loans. This can be helpful in showing your student the impact of borrowing for college vs choosing a lower-cost option.

## Net Price Calculators

In the private college world of highly opaque tuition discounting, your single best tool for researching college costs is the Net Price Calculator (NPC). Every college that participates in the federal student aid programs is required to have an NPC on their website. NPCs allow you to enter your family's financial, and sometimes academic, data and see what students like you received as aid packages the previous school year. And the NPCs have some rules: They can only show gift aid—grants and scholarships—that you would be eligible for without an additional application. They can tell you whether you're likely to be eligible for a subsidized loan or work-study, but they can't include self-help aid (like loans and work-study) in the net price they show you.

Using a few NPCs will show you the range of costs your family is likely to find and how colleges package financial aid, and can certainly help to narrow down your list. My daughter's net price estimates ran up to $81,000 per year; needless to say, she didn't apply to any of those schools. Here's how to get the most out of an NPC:

First you have to find it. Many colleges make them fairly obvious, but not all do. If it's hard to find on the school's website, you can either Google "[school name] net price calculator" or access it via Collegedata, College Navigator, or the Big Future websites by searching the school on those sites.

Next, make sure you're entering your data correctly. For example, income in an NPC is the same as income on the FAFSA: Total income, not AGI. So make sure to add back your pre-tax retirement contributions so as to not understate your income.

The NPC will usually ask you if you want to save your inputs to your student's College Board account. Most parents are horrified at the thought of their student being able to see their incomes and assets, and I get that. However, when you fill out the FAFSA, every line of data in your FAFSA is sent to your student's email address to verify or correct, so not saving your NPC data is only delaying the inevitable. Beyond that, saving your data will save you a ton of time and ensure that every NPC is calculating your estimated net price based on the same set of data.

Most NPCs spit out reasonably detailed estimates that include both your SAI and specific grants and scholarships. What they don't always include are scholarships that require additional applications, although some will list those. My daughter was interested in several schools whose NPCs came in well above her budget; for some of them, she was able to identify additional scholarships that would close the gap between budget and estimated net price. Ultimately, several such schools made her list of colleges to apply to, with the understanding that the additional scholarships would need to be part of the package in order for her to attend.

Keep in mind, too, that NPCs provide **nonbinding estimates** of your net cost. Families whose income varies from year to year might find actual awards to be quite different from quotes provided by NPCs, so it's a good idea to compare the net cost from the NPC with your SAI estimate from the Student Aid Estimator or College Board's EFC estimator. That gives you some indication of the college's markup from your SAI. In our case, each aid award my daughter received was within $2,000 of what the NPC had calculated, but that's not always the case—and it's one more reason why it's important to talk about costs with your student before they get too deep into the process.

## College visits

College visits are a really valuable piece of the research process because, numbers aside, finding your fit really matters. The right fit can be the difference between graduating in four years or five or more—or not finishing college at all. And guess what? You don't have to fly across the country to do great college visits. You can get a ton out of visiting local colleges, even if—or especially if—your student isn't interested in attending any of them because you will see a lot of variation in approaches. For example, how do students engage with the campus' social life? Is there a core curriculum that all students take? Where do students live—on campus or off? Colleges also have fantastic virtual tour options and ways to connect prospective students with students and faculty who can help them in their decision process. Here's a dirty secret: Although I took Gabi on a week-long cross-country college tour, I didn't take Alex on any college visits. He still visited a lot of colleges and is now attending one that he loves. How did we do that?

- Luck: When my two were in middle school and the financial crisis hit, our district added five furlough days to the school year. A group of parents in their class decided to organize academic outings for them. One mom was a professor at a local college, so she arranged a day for them to visit the campus. The kids enjoyed that so much that the class did a college visit each year in middle school. We saw two (very different) small private schools and one big public school—a great intro to the concept of different campus communities.

- Dual-credit courses: Both of my kids took dual-credit math classes, and in those classes they spent a day at the university that granted the credit, including attending the "college" version of their class.

- Traveling: Our families live in different parts of the country, so we've tried to see some colleges when we visit them. And we've occasionally gone to a college while on a vacation.

- Club sports: Alex's soccer team was very focused on getting the boys to play in college, so everywhere outside of Portland that they played games or tournaments, they toured the local colleges with the school's soccer coach and usually met some student athletes. They did this whether they were going to southern Oregon or out of state.

The long and short of it is, you have a lot of opportunities to visit colleges, no matter your circumstances. You could visit local colleges to see the kinds of things you care about. We have four vastly different private colleges in our area that look pretty similar on paper. Touring them helped Gabi to see some of the criteria that mattered to her: Her college needed to be bigger than her high school and needed to actively promote and facilitate student engagement. She also liked the idea of a liberal arts curriculum as part of the academic path. Alex quickly recognized that he wanted a big college experience with football Saturdays and big lectures. None of these criteria were readily apparent to either of them prior to actually setting foot on some college campuses.

One key to doing college visits right—whether you're visiting in person or virtually—is to do an official visit where you sign up with the college. Not only are you demonstrating interest (an important piece of the admissions puzzle at most colleges), but you are likely to find additional opportunities to learn more, such as being put in touch with current students or faculty members in an area of interest.

## Beyond big vs small

When it comes to finding your fit, just big vs small or urban vs rural isn't enough to give you a full picture. Here are some lessons that stuck with us, which we might not have noticed but for talking with a lot of students on our various college visits:

- Asked about what he didn't like about his school, one student mentioned that it's not in a "college town," so although there is a lot happening on campus and in the surrounding community, there isn't a local off-campus, student-oriented gathering place.

- At smaller schools with D-1 sports programs, a significant amount of the social life seems to be oriented around sports.

- Whatever your sport, whatever your level at that sport, most schools will have a place for you to participate with others at the same level. That may or may not be the case for other activities like performing arts.

- At a liberal arts college that is working hard to attract a more diverse student body, one of our tour guides whose family is lower income said she struggled initially to fit in because most of her classmates' families were considerably wealthier than hers and they were accustomed to doing a lot of things in their free time that weren't affordable to her.

- A pre-med student said he chose his school because at all the others he considered, they took great pride in their pre-med course load being "weeder" classes, to weed out the students who couldn't keep up with the demands, whereas the faculty at the school he chose talked more about helping students to succeed in these difficult courses.

- Schools have a range of very different retention tools, based on the priorities they see for their student bodies. These range from student-run social activities or community-building to stress management programs—everything from visiting llamas to free massages to mental health counseling.

- Different schools place different value on engagement with their surrounding communities. Similarly, different communities place different value on their local university and its students being in the community, some embracing the college and others not so much.

- Some schools see housing as a tool for community-building; others use it as a pathway to independence; still others see it primarily as living choices. Some do not permit students to have cars, or limit cars to upperclasspersons.

- Schools have vastly differing policies on alcohol and drug use by students, ranging from "Good Samaritan" policies where students will never be punished for calling for help regardless of their age or state of intoxication, to zero-tolerance zones or policies.

- Colleges see a variety of roles for social organizations like fraternities and sororities or other clubs. Whereas larger campuses tend to encourage most any group that helps students find their place and their people, smaller schools have very different approaches for inclusive and exclusive social groups. These might range from, "We want our students to have access to everything they would have at a big school, so we have a Greek system, sports, theater, clubs... " to "Our campus community is small enough that we don't see a place for exclusive groups."

You and your student will each have your own set of wants. Turn the page for a sample spreadsheet to track and prioritize them.

## WORKSHEET 11: COLLEGE RESEARCH

To download this worksheet, go to howtopayforcollege.com/htpfc-book-worksheets.

Use the following to construct your college research spreadsheet, listing colleges as rows and these prompts as your column headers:

# General information including:

- Website
- Size, location (urban/suburban/rural or other breakdown that matters to you), other demographics of interest to you
- Is the degree/major you're interested in offered?
- Housing information (how long do students live on campus vs off?)
- Quarters or semesters?
- Social considerations that matter to you: athletics, theater, Greek life, academic residential communities, interest groups...

# Application and admissions information including:

- Application deadline
- Application fee and fee waiver eligibility/process
- Letters of Recommendation
- Supplemental essays required?
- Supplemental essay prompts
- Test-optional or test blind?

# Financial information including:

- List price (Cost of Attendance) (from the school's website)
- Expected net price (from net price calculator)

- Is the CSS Profile required?
- Transfer credit policy (will you get credit for your AP/IB/dual-credit classes?)

## Scholarship information including:

- Is merit aid offered?
- Scholarships available that are not reflected in the net price calculator
- Application process and deadline for scholarships
- Top quartile GPA (from Collegedata Admissions tab)
- Top quartile ACT/SAT scores (from Collegedata or College Navigator Admissions tab)
- Are SAT/ACT scores considered for any scholarships?

## Why I would choose this school

- List 1-3 reasons why you would attend this college

## Notes

_____

_____

_____

_____

_____

_____

_____

_____

_____

# CHAPTER 12

# Application Strategies

## WHAT YOU'LL LEARN IN THIS CHAPTER

How to choose where to apply, budgeting for applications, pros and cons of Early Decision and Early Action, and competitive applications.

I F YOUR OWN college application experience involved calling or mailing colleges to request applications, filling out each application by hand, hand-writing your essays, and then trying to figure out how many stamps were required to get the application to its destination on time, you might view the Common App with unbridled joy. Imagine a single application available online that, with a click of a button, can be sent to 10, 20, even 100 colleges!

Gabi initially thought the Common App was like Santa Claus for teenagers: She could write to ask for any future she wanted, and it would bring lots and lots of goodies soon thereafter. As she entered colleges into the Common App, however, the beast's dark underbelly came to light: essay requirements, application fees, test score and CSS Profile submissions, and more. With application fees typically in the $50–$75 range, test scores costing $12 or $16 per request, and $16 for each CSS Profile submission, applying to 10 schools can easily cost $1,000. And no, you can't use your 529 to pay for applications. As a parent who likes to pay my mortgage, feed my family, and keep the lights on in our house, I quickly realized that we needed to cull the herd of "interesting" colleges and set a budget for applications.

Not only is there the cost but also the load of additional work: Many schools require supplemental essays, specific letters of recommendation, scholarship applications, or other time-consuming items. In fact, after we winnowed Gabi's application list down to eight colleges—two of which were public colleges not requiring any additional admission essays—she still had to write more than 20 essays.

## Budgeting for college applications

"Hold on a minute!" you're saying. "You just spent a whole bunch of chapters telling us to cast a wide net for colleges." Yes, you absolutely should cast a wide net in searching for colleges that could be good fits for your student, but that doesn't mean you need to *apply* to each one. In fact, casting a wider net will give you more tools to narrow down your application list to a manageable number.

Plus, having a budget for applications won't just save you money; it will save your student a lot of time and likely make the applications they submit stronger. There is only so much essay writing a teenager can do and still keep up with high school classes and activities, not to mention maintaining the quality of their essays and other application components.

Your application budget will at minimum include the applications themselves. Your student might also be applying to schools that require the CSS Profile; if so, it's $25 for the first submission and $16 for each additional. And your student might have test scores that will benefit them in the admissions process. SAT scores are $12 per request; the ACT charges $16. Plan that you'll average about $100 per application and you'll be able to come up with a cap on application numbers pretty quickly.

There are plenty of ways to bring down your application costs. The Common App offers a fee waiver for students with financial need, which in this context means the student's family receives some form of public assistance such as free or reduced lunch, housing assistance, or the student received a fee waiver for the SAT or ACT; it can even be a letter from their high school stating the student's need.

Most colleges want more applicants—it makes them more selective—so most will offer fee waivers based on various criteria, both economic or non-economic. Some offer fee waivers to any student who submits a FAFSA; others to students who have toured the school, including virtually. Some waive fees for students who apply before a cutoff date. It's always worth asking the school what its fee waiver criteria are.

You should also have a plan for your test score submissions, since most colleges are test-optional. Generally speaking, it only makes sense to submit test scores if they're good relative to the college's current student body. Students can look up test score ranges for each college on Collegedata or College Navigator and decide on a school-by-school basis whether to submit test scores. Unfortunately there's very little consistency in how test-optional colleges treat test submissions. A number of colleges—especially private ones—admit much higher percentages of students who did submit scores than of those who did not; at other colleges, the admission rates are fairly equal among test-submitters and non-submitters. At colleges that make a holistic application review, test scores might be less significant when the student's overall application is stronger, but could help students (like my son) who might be late bloomers in the classroom. The bottom line is, not every college needs to see your test scores.

Here's a pro tip: You can absolutely bring down the cost of applications, but that does *not* mean that you should add an additional college to your application list just because you secure a fee waiver. Each application takes time, in addition to money, and time is a finite resource for a high school senior. Having more of it will mean not just that they can improve the quality of their applications, but also that they can be present in the moments their senior year offers rather than focusing exclusively on the future.

## The Common App

Again, no one writes to schools to request applications any more. Instead, most colleges participate in the Common App. The Common App is a single application system that sends the student's application to multiple colleges of their choice. The student creates an account, selects the colleges to which they'll apply, uploads their data—high school transcript, test scores, activities, responsibilities, awards and more—and the Common App loads all of the application requirements—supplemental essays, letters of recommendation, standardized test requirements—so that the student can manage everything in one place.

Virtually every participating college requires the Common App's essay. Students select one of several essay prompts to write about themselves. These prompts are quite consistent year-to-year and can be found on the Common App's website.

Each college has its own information page within the Common App, where students can see what additional materials the college requires. For example, most private colleges require applicants to write two additional essays, each of which is unique to the school. Going through the list of supplemental essays can be a helpful exercise in winnowing down your list of college choices. Many require letters of recommendation, and some specify which teacher(s) should write those. For example, students applying to engineering or other STEM programs may need to provide a letter of rec from a STEM subject teacher.

Students submit their application materials and pay application fees to colleges through the Common App. Test scores, the FAFSA and CSS

Profile submissions are done directly through those entities, although the Common App will give guidance on what each school requires.

The Common App also offers a fee waiver program where eligible students can request a blanket fee waiver, or gain individual fee waivers from colleges. The blanket Common App fee waiver requires a letter from the student's high school counselor attesting to financial need. Students can also reach out directly to colleges and request fee waivers; many are happy to oblige, so it never hurts to ask.

Not all colleges participate in the Common App, although most do. Because the list of participating colleges grows every year, you're better off just checking whether the schools you're considering accept it, rather than having me put a list here. In addition, there are other application aggregation platforms including the Coalition App and the Common Black College Application, though each of those is accepted at a smaller number of schools. Good news: A lot of your Common App materials will still be usable for non-Common App applications, though it's time consuming to re-upload them, or to convert a 650-word essay to a 500-word essay.

And again, while the Common App makes it easy to apply to many colleges, the fact that you can doesn't necessarily mean that you should. Each application takes a combination of time and money, both of which are finite resources.

## Narrowing down your list

Before you apply to any college, it has to pass the "Why would I go here?" test. Let's say your student has 15 colleges they're interested in and your goal is to bring that down to 10. Maybe a handful are academic reaches—highly competitive schools where your odds of admission are similar to your odds of getting one of Willy Wonka's golden tickets. Then you've got your in-state public school. You have about five slots left.

If you didn't complete the net price calculators for those schools in the worksheet from the last chapter, do them now—that might rule out a couple. If any school doesn't offer a path to affordability, between its net price calculator, additional scholarships you might be eligible for, and outside scholarships you plan to apply for, cross it off your list now.

By all means, have your student apply to a "safety" school—one where they're reasonably certain to not just get in but also to get a financial aid and scholarship package that works for your budget. But you don't need to apply to three safety schools; one is fine.

Our family's decision tree was pretty straightforward. Gabi wanted to go out of state, and we felt like a private school would be the best fit for her, but she had great scholarship opportunities at our in-state flagship school and a neighboring state's flagship school. She wanted an urban environment and gravitated to Boston and Chicago, loving every school we visited in both cities; she ruled out New York after visiting her cousin there and determining it's a great place to visit but not where she wanted to live.

We knocked her Boston applications down to three by ruling out two that would never meet our budget. We picked only one Boston safety school and then her two top choices, where admissions were very competitive. Besides the three Boston schools, she also applied to two Chicago schools, plus her uncle's Ivy League alma mater, and the two close-by flagship public schools, for a total of eight.

Four of her schools had single-digit acceptance rates, so she knew that she couldn't count on any of them. A fifth was slightly less competitive; the sixth was a shoo-in for admissions and had a reasonable scholarship path for her. Our in-state school was her last choice, but best financial opportunity. The neighboring state's public school has a great program in her desired field, would be reasonable financially with the help of scholarships, and was a sufficiently better fit than our in-state school that we would all be OK with her enrolling there.

# Give yourself the tools to negotiate

One strategy that can be helpful in getting more financial aid from your top choice school is applying to an academic peer school that's likely to give you a better aid offer. ("But hang on! You just told us we should apply to fewer schools!" I know, but hear me out on this.) If a student is accepted to both schools, the better financial aid award can be used to negotiate for more aid at the student's top choice school. Think of it like asking for a raise at work: Your negotiating position is stronger if you have another job offer at higher pay. How do you find academic peers who are likely to give better awards? You research their financial aid and scholarship policies, including using net price calculators.

For example, your top choice college might use the CSS Profile, but you might be able to find a similar college that uses the FAFSA. Most students have a lower SAI on the FAFSA than on the CSS Profile, so applying to one of your top choice's peers that uses the FAFSA might result in a better financial aid award, which can be used to negotiate with the top choice school. Of course, this depends on the student being accepted to both colleges. Examples of private colleges that use the FAFSA include the University of Chicago, Puget Sound, and Gonzaga. In addition, the College Board's website shows nuances in data used by Profile schools, such as many that only require one divorced parent—not both—to report income and assets.

The most selective colleges—the "Ivy-Plus" schools such as Yale, Stanford, the University of Chicago, and so on—are typically extremely generous with need-based financial aid (in contrast to their stance on merit-based aid). That's because one way they keep admissions so competitive is by making sure that accepted students don't have any reason not to enroll. Furthermore, their most generous grants are often based on household income, not the FAFSA or CSS Profile. For example, students whose family income is below a certain threshold would get full scholarships; those at a slightly higher threshold would get full-tuition scholarships. If your student is an academic high achiever and your household income falls within one of those bands, which you can find on the schools' websites, your student would do well to apply there. Not only might they get a generous financial aid award if accepted, they could also use that aid award to negotiate with other schools to which they're accepted.

Students can use search tools like Collegedata and the College Board's Big Future website to find comparable schools with different aid and scholarship policies by using the search criteria—size, location, admissions data—to find alternatives. And who knows: Maybe you'll find some great options that you weren't even considering.

You don't necessarily need a competitor for every college you're applying to; one or two competitors is plenty. But the schools need to be truly comparable. Private colleges generally don't care what a public college offered you, and a more selective college won't typically care what a less selective one offered. For example, Santa Clara might be more willing to match Stanford's financial aid award than vice versa.

## Should you apply early?

Early Decision (ED) and Early Action (EA) are important considerations for students. EA is simply applying early to a college— usually by November 1 instead of January 1—and getting an answer from the college early, typically by mid-December. Students accepted via EA have until the standard May 1 enrollment deadline to accept or decline admission.

EA is in many cases more of a convenience for students who are ready to apply sooner rather than later. However, some colleges offer a form of EA called rolling admissions, in which applications are considered as they are received. In the case of rolling admissions, financial aid awards are also often granted in the order in which the application (and

FAFSA) are received and funds may run out, so it's usually beneficial to apply as early as possible to a college offering rolling admissions.

ED, on the other hand, is an early application and answer on a similar timeline with EA, with one major difference: It's a binding commitment to attend the college if you are accepted. Students can only apply ED to a single college, and in fact some groups of colleges compare lists of students who have applied ED to confirm that students are not submitting multiple applications.

The decision whether to apply ED has two components: The admissions piece and the financial piece. Plenty of schools admit a higher percentage of applicants via ED than in the regular admissions cycle; however, the students who are admitted via ED don't necessarily have different credentials than those admitted in regular decision. That means that applying ED to a reach school is likely to be an exercise in frustration; if you're not in the academic range of the students the college enrolls, you're not any more likely to get in via ED than via regular decision.

ED is very different for students with financial need. Since you can only apply to one college in the ED cycle, you won't have any leverage to negotiate the financial aid offer other than to decline admission if the financial package you get isn't sufficient. So if money matters, you should not apply ED.

It's a little different for athletes. Most coaches want athletes to apply ED and most will be helpful in getting good financial aid and merit scholarship estimates from the school in advance of applying, if you just ask.

## Community college: Your insurance policy

A final piece of your application strategy is your insurance policy: Community college. Where free community college is offered, it often comes with a caveat: Students need to apply for it while in high school.

Students enrolled at four-year colleges often find themselves spending a term or more at community college, for a variety of reasons: Illness, a gap before a transfer, study abroad or gap year programs that don't align with their college's academic calendar. And that doesn't even factor in global pandemics.

Further, dual enrollment programs—where a student is simultaneously enrolled in a four-year college and its neighboring community college—often allow free community college enrollment. That means a student can have a four-year college "experience" while completing two years of courses tuition-free at a community college.

Almost all free community college programs have restrictions, whether simply that you must apply while in high school or income thresholds above which a student is not eligible. Now is the time to learn about your state's program so that your student can apply. Again, think of this as an insurance policy in the event your student ends up spending some time at a community college. In my neighborhood, of the 15 students who have gone off to four-year colleges in recent years, five have spent some unanticipated time at community college along the way. And those who had applied for Oregon Promise (our state's free community college program) while in high school were able to complete some credits for free.

## Getting outside help

What else needs to factor into your application budget? Many families also hire help with the process: Test preparation, admissions consultants, and essay coaches are among the many potentially costly resources out there. Any of these services can range in cost up to thousands of dollars, depending on the nature of the resources being offered and regional pricing differences.

In each of these cases, these resources can be a good investment if they help your student find better scholarships and better fits.

Unfortunately for families, "college advisors" are a lot like "financial advisors" insofar as thousands of people performing myriad different services call themselves the same thing. This means it's important to identify your needs in the admissions process before looking for help, and to develop a budget and lay out your specific goals for that help. Plenty of families—most families, really—navigate the process without extra help or by using DIY tools like this book that provide resources for identifying and selecting schools that could work for your student.

Students who have a good handle on where they're going to apply and whether those schools will fit their budget might need help with specific aspects of the process such as essay writing, test preparation, or just general project management—because applying to college can be a huge project. Students with specific college goals, such as learning environments or opportunities to pursue sports at the collegiate level, might benefit from working with a consultant with expertise in their particular area of interest. Most consultants are independent, meaning that families wanting to hire a college consultant need to use a combination of word-of-mouth recommendations and due diligence to find a good one. Actual college consultants—not the Rick Singers of the world—usually belong to at least one of several professional associations: IECA (the Independent Educational Consulting Association), HECA (the Higher Education Consultants Association) or NCAG (the National College Advocacy Group), all of which have admissions and ethics standards, as well as continuing education requirements. That's not to say that you won't find good independent consultants who aren't a member of one of these, but it does mean buyer beware.

Before choosing to work with a professional in the admissions process, make sure you're clear about your needs and goals in doing so. Gabi knew which colleges she was going to apply to. When we looked at the essay requirements and her senior year fall schedule—a full IB courseload, a role in the fall play, and a part-time job—and her typical teenager not-very-awesome project management skills, we decided to hire an essay coach. I called her our Winter Break Vacation Insurance, since our goal was that all college applications would be submitted before winter break. Alex, on the other hand, was only interested in big public colleges in the West that would cost the same as staying in-state. This was a pretty small pool that he could find on his own, and he ended up applying to two colleges for which he only needed the standard Common App and no supplemental materials. Bonus: His high school English class wrote Common App essays during the fall, so he was able to pull together everything he needed to apply to college without our help.

Ready to narrow down your list? Turn the page for a worksheet on "why would my student go here?"

## WORKSHEET 12: WHY WOULD MY STUDENT GO HERE?

To download this worksheet, go to howtopayforcollege.com/htpfc-book-worksheets.

My application budget:                                                    $ _____

Divide by 100 for number of colleges to apply to:               _____

**Exercise 1**: Rank all the colleges in the college selection worksheet (previous chapter) in order of preference: If your student were accepted to every one, which would they go to?

_____

**Exercise 2**: After completing net price calculators and researching scholarships available at each school, eliminate all colleges that don't meet your budget.

_____

**Exercise 3**: The Green group. Identify your financial safety school: The one that you can afford, no matter what, and that will offer your student admission. If more than one meet those criteria, rank them in order of preference.

_____

**Exercise 4**: The Yellow group. Identify the colleges you're confident your student will be accepted to. Rank them in order of preference, noting expected net price.

---

**Exercise 5**: The Red group. The remaining colleges are your academic "reach" schools where you're not confident of admission, but likely to accept if admitted. Rank them in order of preference, noting expected net price.

---

**Exercise 6**: Start your list. Put your top choice school from each group on your list. Then ask yourself, "What would prevent my student from going here?" That will give you some guidance on how to fill the remaining slots on your list. For example, if you would need to get a highly competitive scholarship to attend your Red or Yellow list school, add another school from that list that has a more likely financial path. Or if all of your top choices are far away (or close to home), add one that's closer (or away if that is a goal). Your goal here is to fill holes so that whatever set of acceptances your student gets, you have good choices.

---

**Exercise 7**: Finish your list. Continue adding to your list from Exercise 6 by going through each remaining college in order and asking yourself about each, "Why would my student go here?" If you come up with an answer that isn't addressed by another college on the list and you still have spots on your list to fill, add this one.

---

# CHAPTER 13

# Reviewing Financial Aid Awards

## WHAT YOU'LL LEARN IN THIS CHAPTER

How to figure out what a college really costs, how to compare aid awards accurately, how to negotiate for more money.

YOU MIGHT RECALL that Alex applied to—and was accepted by—two colleges: the University of Oregon and the University of Arizona. Arizona offered him a generous scholarship; nonetheless, when we compared bottom-line numbers on the two financial aid awards, Arizona looked to be $7,000 more expensive. Each year.

While I love my son dearly and was incredibly proud of him for looking beyond what's familiar and finding a college where he was eligible for a big scholarship, $7,000 seemed like a lot to spend for nicer weather. He disagreed. As we discussed the cost difference, he was the human manifestation of wind coming out of the sails: Slumped, dejected, quiet—a stark contrast to his normal upbeat self. And honestly, we liked the version of him that was interested in Arizona. When he talked about going to Arizona, it was about living in the academic residential community for business majors and signing up for intramurals as a free agent to meet more people and get more connected with the campus community—or thinking about how to choose a roommate when he didn't know anyone. When he talked about going to Oregon, it was "Kevin said I should live in this dorm" and "I guess I'll be roommates with Mateus." But $7,000 a year is a big number—and after four years it's $28,000. Not to mention travel costs.

"We're on your side," we told him, "but you're asking for almost $30,000 extra for better weather." We told him that if he could bring the cost of attendance at Arizona in line with the cost at Oregon, he would have our full support in choosing to go there. So off he went on a research expedition, where he learned some really fascinating things.

## What goes into cost of attendance

Colleges have very different approaches to calculating cost of attendance. Operating on the principle that students can only borrow up to the stated cost of attendance, many colleges that have different price tiers for housing and meal plans quote cheaper options in cost of attendance because doing so limits borrowing. Others operate on the principle that scholarships and financial aid can only cover the cost of attendance and thus include more expensive housing and meal plans and sometimes even extras like health insurance in the cost of attendance. Books, personal expenses, and other items included in cost of attendance similarly vary tremendously by school.

Such was the case with Alex's two schools. As it turned out, Oregon used low housing and meal costs, whereas Arizona used higher ones. So Oregon was going to cost about $2,000 more than was quoted in cost of attendance, and he was plenty willing to choose a cheaper dorm at Arizona if that made it possible for him to attend. He very quickly closed $4,500 of the annual gap.

Next he learned that Arizona guarantees students the same tuition rate for all four years. Here in Oregon, annual tuition increases are usually in the 5% range. (Since then, Oregon has also implemented guaranteed tuition for four years.) Five percent of $14,000 is $700, so by senior year we could expect his cost to be the same at both schools. He also learned that typical apartment rents are cheaper in Tucson than in Eugene, and saving $100–$200 per month on rent adds up pretty quickly.

Finally, he was told that Arizona typically has a shortage of male RAs for the dorms, so a high percentage of male applicants get hired. As a former camp counselor, he felt that being an RA would be a pretty good fit for him, and would provide a year of free room and board.

All in all, he was able to make his top choice school cost the same or even less than another option that on the surface seemed considerably cheaper. I'm so glad he could do that, because he has really thrived in his new environment, going from an apathetic high school student to a straight-As college student; forging some great relationships with fellow students, faculty, and advisors; and developing a level of independence and self-confidence I'm not convinced he would have if he'd chosen the more comfortable path of staying local.

## The award letter

College acceptance letters typically come with financial aid and scholarship awards, so you know when you're accepted what your award package looks like. But comparing award letters from different schools might seem like comparing apples to taco salad. The good news is, all offers need to show total cost of attendance, gift aid offered, and any self-help aid—work-study and loans, as applicable. Unfortunately, they have pretty broad latitude in how they do it. And really, there are two pieces to comparing college costs: What's in the award letter and what's in the school's cost of attendance.

As you're reviewing award letters, it's easy to get caught up in the size of scholarships being offered. But remember that your goal is to figure out what your actual annual out-of-pocket cost to attend would be. It's not always the case that the college offering the biggest scholarship is the cheapest.

Let's start with the award letter, since that's the easy part. The award letter will show—usually at the top—the total cost of attendance before any aid is subtracted. Gift aid usually comes next and can have multiple components. Then the award letter will state whether the student is eligible for work-study or subsidized loans; in addition, it may include an unsubsidized Direct Student Loan. Then, the student's net cost will be listed. Your job in reviewing award letters is to remove the "self-help" aid—loans and work-study—to figure out your actual out-of-pocket cost. When doing this, double-check whether the aid amounts are listed annually or by academic term. (Don't worry, there's a worksheet at the end of this chapter.)

Once you've subtracted your gift aid from cost of attendance, you have a good starting point. But the next thing to figure out is what's included in the cost of attendance. This is tricky because as noted earlier, schools have a lot of latitude in what they include in cost of attendance and thus could show very high or very low numbers relative to actual cost.

## How do you compare?

In order to make apples-to-apples comparisons, you need to find out a few things:

- Do you have options with housing costs or meal plans? If so, check out your options rather than just assuming what's in your award letter is what you want. In Alex's case, once we "standardized" the room and board costs based on what he would actually choose, we closed a sizable gap between his two schools.

- Can you opt out of any of the cost of attendance items? Gabi's school includes the student health insurance plan in the cost of attendance; it's waived with proof of insurance. This makes her school almost $5,000 cheaper annually than the published cost.

- Books and personal expenses likely have little to do with what's listed. Gabi's school quotes $3,000 annually for books; Alex's says $800. Neither of those is correct, though for some majors they could be close. Some colleges are now moving toward all-online books, which does make it easier to get accurate cost estimates. Majors that rely heavily on textbooks or lab supplies will have higher costs.

- For schools that are not local, figure out what your annual travel budget looks like. Your student will travel to campus in the fall, may come home at Thanksgiving, will make a roundtrip for winter break and likely spring break, and then come home for the summer. Your budget should also include a family visit to campus if that's something you'd want to do.

One good way to get a handle on these types of costs is to ask the college to put you in touch with a current student. Another is to join the Facebook parents' page for the college. These can be a wealth of information and you'll typically find plenty of people who will be generous in sharing their knowledge and experiences on a wide range of topics. (Your student will likely be invited to join an admitted students' group, which is a great way to see who they might be going to college with, but those fellow admitted students are not likely to know any more than yours does about college costs.)

Your final step in reviewing financial aid awards is to compare them with your college budget. Pull out the spreadsheet you created in Chapter 10 and update the numbers with your current savings balance, your and your student's contributions from income, and any scholarships your student has earned. You'll add this information into this chapter's worksheet so you can see whether your choices are affordable for your family or if there are gaps to close. With that information, you can finalize your cost comparison spreadsheet so that you are truly comparing apples to apples.

## Scholarship renewal

Perhaps the most important consideration with your financial aid award is whether and how the scholarships are renewable. For this, it matters whether they're merit- or need-based.

Merit scholarships generally have set criteria for renewal, and as long as the student hits those criteria, they keep their scholarship. Typical is a 3.0 GPA and full-time enrollment, but each school sets its own policies so it's best to confirm.

Need-based awards, including work-study and subsidized loans, are recalculated every year based on that year's FAFSA or CSS Profile. Families with need-based awards should be mindful of components of that calculation:

- The family's income and assets. Parents whose income varies from year to year might have had a lower-income year in their first FAFSA and might learn that their aid package will change significantly in the coming year.

- The number of students in college. Even with this being eliminated from the FAFSA, it remains a consideration on the CSS Profile and for many colleges in disbursing institutional aid. If your student has multiple older siblings in college, their package will probably look different—smaller—once those siblings graduate.

- Household size. As above, if older siblings graduate and become independent, the household size reported on the FAFSA will be smaller, resulting in a smaller income protection allowance.

- Formula changes. If your first FAFSA was pre-Simplification and any of the FAFSA Simplification changes impact you— particularly for students whose parents are divorced or who have multiple siblings in college—you should be mindful of that. While many colleges will continue considering these elements in offering institutional aid, they are under no obligation to do so—and students may lose out on federal funds including Pell Grants, work-study or subsidized loans.

You can use net price calculators to estimate your aid package under different scenarios. Your best bet, however, is to contact the financial aid office at your top choice college(s) and ask them to run through the scenarios with you. In the case of FAFSA Simplification changes, you should also ask the college to confirm (in writing) that they will continue to calculate your aid package based on the previous formula.

And again, if it isn't in writing on the award letter, confirm with the college what's required to renew your award every year.

## Other cost factors

You should also research other factors that will impact your costs, like college location or student demographics. Colleges in urban, especially coastal, locations will generally have higher room and board costs simply due to the higher cost of living in those areas. This is especially the case for students who live off campus.

Students intending to participate in study abroad should research how their aid package works during study abroad. Even if a school says "Your aid package goes with you," that could mean that your scholarship stays the same and you're responsible for incremental costs, or that your net cost stays the same despite incremental costs. In either case, the student is almost always responsible for travel costs associated with study abroad.

Social life plays a big role in costs. At campuses where the social life revolves around on-campus housing or activities, students usually have plenty of options to engage without extra out-of-pocket costs.

Is Greek life a big part of the campus social life? If your student intends to participate, that should be part of your budget. Dues might run from $250 to $750 per academic term; activity fees often come on top of that. In addition, most fraternities and sororities have social functions requiring formal or semi-formal dress, and members tend to buy a lot of swag like t-shirts and sweatshirts.

Micro-location factors can play a role, too. Many campuses have fast food or coffee shops either in or adjacent to dorms. Often you see 75% or more of students on their way to class clutching a coffee or juice. An extra $4 per day for food that isn't part of your meal plan adds up pretty quickly.

And then there are student demographics. A friend's daughter, who attends a small private college where many students come from affluent families, complained that her friends went out to restaurants for dinner several times a week rather than eating on campus and that, as a result, she was going through her savings far more quickly than she had anticipated. She eventually found some on-campus activities to join that made her unavailable several evenings a week and made a plan to eat on campus before going out with friends, but peer pressure can be a challenging source of extra expenses for many students.

## Who is responsible for which costs?

The point at which you review aid awards is a great time to reconfirm with your student what skin you expect them to have in the game. Not only is it simply being fair to your student, it might help avoid some buyer's remorse if you clarify expectations and put numbers around them before they choose.

There is no single "correct" division of cost between students and parents, though as a financial advisor, I feel strongly that college is too big of an investment to be shouldered by one party—whether parents or students—alone. Any student should be able to contribute something to their education; that amount is for your family to map out. Here are some thoughts.

## Specific line items

You might ask your student to be responsible for specific pieces of their college cost. This can be helpful in ensuring that they make good choices about textbooks or meal plans, for example, or to reinforce additional travel costs resulting from choosing an out-of-state college. If you go this route, make sure that they have a way of getting the money in the timeframe it's needed. A student who is responsible for their own books will need to arrive at school with the funds required, since most books need to be bought early in the term.

Likewise, be careful about assigning costs in which you have a vested interest to your student. For example, if you place a high value on having your family together at Thanksgiving, you should not make your student responsible for their travel-home budget or you are likely to be disappointed.

## A specific dollar amount

The worksheet provided has a line for a dollar amount for the student to contribute from cash flow, because that makes sense from a budgeting perspective and gives the student a target income from part-time or summer jobs. If you go this route, be clear with your student what that dollar amount applies to. For example, if you expect them to contribute $3,000 annually, does that mean paying a portion of their direct expenses like tuition or room and board? Or are you budgeting that for indirect expenses like their personal spending money?

## A percentage of the total

This strategy can be helpful in getting your student invested in managing costs, since no one likes a moving target. A student who's responsible for 10% of their college costs has a different nut to crack depending on whether their college costs $25,000 annually or $65,000. Not only that, but it can help guide conversations around room and board choices.

## Any amount above the parents' budget

Your budget may be fixed; if so, your student might be responsible for the rest of the cost. Again, this is an opportunity to help your student make good choices about where they invest their money, since college is an investment. If your budget is $20,000 annually and your student's top choice college is $60,000, they should be giving their second and third choices a better look, considering what $160,000 in student loan debt would feel like. They may also need to consider appealing their financial aid award, and maybe just crossing that school off their list.

Your job as the parent is to make sure that your student can come up with their contribution in a reasonable fashion: Whether through part-time and summer work, reasonable borrowing (the Direct Student Loan) or a combination of the two. You also need to be clear about when their portion is due, how it is to be paid, and what the consequences of not paying are. For example, if your student is responsible for a portion of tuition, they need to have that money available for you before tuition is due or take out a Direct Student Loan. Students responsible for their own rent or utility payments should also understand the credit report consequences of nonpayment; you can help them set up autopay to manage that.

One big reason for your student to have some skin in the game is also a big reason for students to go to college in the first place: To develop the skills to succeed in the world as independent adults. Giving them responsibility for a portion of their costs and working with them to make sure they live up to that responsibility is not punitive: It's good parenting.

My two kids are responsible for their personal expenses like clothes, social life and food costs above their meal plan or budget, as well as their books. In addition, since they are attending their top choice colleges on the basis of having received scholarships that made those colleges fit our budget, they are responsible for keeping their scholarships or funding the difference. They are also responsible for all fees that could be waived, since they are the ones filing the fee waiver. We wanted them to be able to focus completely on college their first year, so they had to earn enough over the summer before college started to cover their expected expenses for the first year without taking on a part-time job.

Because I want to make sure they learn good money skills and don't inadvertently trash their credit ratings, I also set up an online savings account for each, which both of us have access to. They transferred their money for the year into the savings account, then we set up periodic transfers into their personal bank accounts to help their money last for the year. Now that Alex lives in an apartment, he gets a monthly transfer for rent shortly before rent is due, along with a monthly transfer for food. His apartment building, which is university-owned, gives parents the option to be notified of payment due dates and status. Needless to say, we chose that option.

## Appealing your financial aid award

People negotiate most big things in life. It's rare not to negotiate when buying a home or a car or when you're offered a new job. And yet, comparatively few students or families negotiate their financial aid awards. Whether that's because we think we should just be thankful our student was admitted or grateful for the package that was given, colleges are the winner when you don't appeal. Many families can save thousands of dollars by appealing their financial aid award. Remind yourself: If a college has admitted your student, the college wants them to attend. It costs the college less to increase your aid package than to have your student go elsewhere.

## Appealing a need-based award

To be effective, you need to understand the process, which is different depending on what aid you have. The process for need-based aid is called Professional Judgment, or PJ. In this case, the school has a specific set of constraints and you must work within them. The Department of Education allows schools to make adjustments "on a case-by-case basis only to adjust the student's cost of attendance or the data used to calculate her [SAI]." What that means is, the school can adjust elements of the student's data that are used to calculate SAI, but not the SAI calculation itself. And the school can adjust the student's cost of attendance by increasing the amount for categories like room and board, books, or personal expenses.

The reasons for adjustment "must relate to the special circumstances that differentiate [the student]—not to conditions that exist for a whole class of students." In many cases, the family's financial situation has changed since the tax return that was used for the FAFSA or CSS Profile. This might include a job loss or change, medical expenses, a parent going back to school, or even unusual childcare expenses. In any such circumstances, the school is allowed to recalculate the student's SAI on the basis of new information.

Included in the above are one-time gains during the income year used for the FAFSA that might have caused the family's income to be higher in the base year than is typically the case. This might include a bonus, a stock grant, a withdrawal or Roth conversion from an IRA account, or a one-time capital gain.

Families with incomes that vary from year to year can use this to their advantage: If your income in the base year for your FAFSA was higher than typical, you can appeal your aid award based on the subsequent year's income—and then use that income for a second year since it will be the next year's FAFSA income. For example, a parent who earns commissions might earn $120,000 in one year and $80,000 the next year. The student could appeal their award on the basis that the parent's income is $40,000 less in the current year than it was in the year used for the FAFSA. And then that $80,000 income year will be used for the subsequent FAFSA, too.

Colleges may also offer some leeway in treatment of assets. A family with significant assets in non-retirement accounts might make the case that those assets are retirement assets if there's a reason that they are not in retirement accounts. Reasons might include limited or no access to an employer retirement account or a one-time payout received for selling a business at retirement.

Any change made through the PJ process needs to be supported in writing, with documentation. So be prepared to produce documents like severance letters, documentation of unemployment compensation, medical records, or whatever item is pertinent.

Remember, too, that aid awards are subject to the school's aid packaging, which may include loans and work-study in addition to grants. So a student who initially did not receive any aid might appeal and receive a Direct Student Loan or work-study as their aid award. However, once a student has been accepted to a college, the college typically wants them to attend and will often help meet additional gaps.

When appealing an aid award that is based on your SAI, you need to do the following:

- Document, in writing, the circumstances your family faces that would change your SAI.

- Do not request a specific dollar amount. The administrator can only change the formula inputs, not the formula itself.

- Start the process as soon after receiving an award as possible. That's because there is typically a fixed pool of need-based funds, and you want to ask for some while they're still available.

- Because the adjustment to a need-based award is school-specific, a better offer from a different school may factor into a school's willingness to negotiate or adjust on your behalf, but is no guarantee either that the school will negotiate or that they will match the other school's offer.

## Appealing for more merit

Merit awards offer schools far more flexibility, and if your top choice college awards merit, you can go back and ask for merit aid if they didn't offer you any in their initial letter. Again, remember that any college that admitted your student probably wants to enroll them, so don't hesitate to ask.

Here are some steps you can take to increase your chances on a merit aid appeal:

- Research the school's merit aid policies so that you are approaching the appeal based on the school's policies. For example, a student who finds that a nominally higher GPA would have yielded a much larger scholarship might appeal on the basis of having chosen a more academically rigorous high school courseload.

- Research the school's overall financial aid policies and awards on a site like the College Board or Collegedata and where your student fits academically within the student population. That will give you a sense of what the school offers and whether you're the type of student to whom it's offered.

- Provide copies of aid awards from other, comparable schools who are offering you more. Many colleges will happily provide $2,000–$3,000 extra if they have reason to believe that will get you to accept and come on board for the next four years.

- Appeal in writing, with a polite letter that both expresses gratitude for what's already been offered and provides a detailed rationale for why you deserve more.

In either case—PJ or a request for additional merit aid—the appeal should be done in writing, signed by the student.

## Negotiation in general

Besides understanding the process for appealing, you should think about negotiation in general before you go into this process. Here are some negotiation basics that often seem to fall by the wayside in negotiating aid offers:

- What is your goal in the process? Even when you aren't presenting an aid administrator with a dollar goal, you should have one in mind based on the college cash flow plan you've created. You should understand what is affordable for your family and whether you're willing to stretch that by some specific amount for one or another school.

- What will you do if you don't get what you want? At what point do you walk away? You and your student should know going into the negotiating process what you will accept and what would be insufficient, leading you to choose "plan B."

- What's your alternative? If you don't get a better offer, do you have a financial safety school? Does the dream school have a path that includes community college for a couple of quarters or semesters?

For schools, the aid process is a business decision. There are a certain number of dollars available in grants and loans, and they will be allocated in a certain way across the student body based on a set of goals and values. Families need to look at the process in the same way and use a clear-headed approach to negotiation that includes the possibility of walking away. If you know your budget, your options, and your goals going into the process, you're far more likely to get to an outcome that works for your family.

The final piece of appealing financial aid awards is this: You can do it at any time during your college years. If your family's situation changes—a job loss, illness or anything else with financial repercussions—reach out to your school's financial aid office immediately. While there's no guarantee that anything will change, most colleges do want to keep students enrolled and many are willing to work with families through hardships.

Got that? Turn the page for a worksheet on comparing college costs.

# WORKSHEET 13: COLLEGE COST COMPARISON

To download this worksheet, go to howtopayforcollege.com/htpfc-book-worksheets.

| | (name of college) | (name of college) | (name of college) |
|---|---|---|---|
| **Cost of Attendance** | $ | $ | $ |
| **Total Grants** | $ | $ | $ |
| **Total Scholarships** | $ | $ | $ |
| **Net Price (After Grants & Scholarships)** | $ | $ | $ |

**Adjustments**

| | | | |
|---|---|---|---|
| Adjust for Housing Cost | $ | $ | $ |
| Adjust for Meal Plan Cost | $ | $ | $ |
| Adjust for Travel Cost | $ | $ | $ |
| Other Adjustments | $ | $ | $ |
| Total Adjustments | $ | $ | $ |
| **Adjusted Est. Net Price** | $ | $ | $ |
| Annual Family Contribution | $ | $ | $ |
| **Annual Shortfall Before Self-Help** | $ | $ | $ |

**Self-Help Aid**

| | | | |
|---|---|---|---|
| Work-Study | $ | $ | $ |
| Direct Student Loans | $ | $ | $ |
| **Total Self-Help Aid** | $ | $ | $ |
| **Total Annual Shortfall** | $ | $ | $ |

# CHAPTER 14

# Developing a Cash Flow Plan

## WHAT YOU'LL LEARN IN THIS CHAPTER

How to spend down assets to maximize other benefits, how to withdraw from your 529, when college bills are due.

M Y UNCLE SAID that kids getting braces was good practice for college—you open up your wallet and hand over everything in it. My financial advisor self would tell you it's more that paying for college is good practice for retirement: Time to change your mindset from saving to responsible spending. Whatever your feelings on the subject, once your student accepts at a school, the rubber meets the road. Now all of that saving you've done gets flipped on its head and you start to spend. It can be scary, after years of saving!

After Alex and Gabi accepted at their schools, the whole family was bombarded with decisions: Go to orientation or skip it? (Sometimes it's required; other times just strongly encouraged.) Which dorm? Which meal plan? Choose a roommate or get assigned a roommate? Which roommate rents the minifridge? How long do we stay at drop-off? What do they need to bring? (On this point, timing is everything. Alex left for Arizona in late August, and we were planning to come to parents' weekend in mid-October. That meant he mostly needed shorts and t-shirts, and we could bring some long pants and sweatshirts later. Gabi, on the other hand, went to Chicago at the end of September, so even though we planned to come for parents' weekend about a month later, we knew she could experience at least three seasons in that first month.) Do you ship their things in advance or bring everything when they first move in?

As you're in the throes of all these decisions—including the internal dialogue of how much to insert yourself into decisions that are really your student's to make—you get a bill from the college. How are you going to pay for it?

## The nitty-gritty payment details

Let's start with the basics of what you pay, and when you need to pay it. The first payment you'll be required to make is your deposit. This is due when your student accepts admission. Deposits are usually in the $200–$500 range, depending on the college, and are nonrefundable—something for waitlisted students to keep in mind.

Many colleges charge additional deposits for dorm assignments; these are usually due as soon as the student makes a housing selection, regardless of whether they've accepted admission. Many students choose to pay the housing deposit as soon as possible—in some cases, even before they accept admission—in order to secure their top housing choice. Dorm deposits tend to be refundable; however, in the wake of the pandemic, many colleges have tightened refund policies as a means to shore up budgets.

Tuition, fees and on-campus room and board are billed just prior to the start of the academic term. They are usually divided equally across academic terms, whether that's quarters or semesters. Colleges send out a statement in advance showing actual costs. When you compare these to your financial aid award, the costs on the statement will usually be higher. That's because most colleges haven't set their costs for the coming school year when acceptances and aid awards are sent out, so those awards are based on then-current costs. Financial aid and scholarships may or may not be included in the initial statement. We often don't see the actual amount we owe until a few days before it's due.

You should check the initial statement for any items that can be waived and reach out to the college immediately for waiver instructions. For example, Gabi's college includes student health insurance and a public transit pass in cost of attendance; insurance is waived if the student provides proof of insurance, but the transit pass can only be waived in certain circumstances (the pandemic was one of them).

Outside scholarships are disbursed directly to the college and divided equally across academic terms. Colleges are required to reduce need-based aid by 50 cents per dollar of outside scholarship. However, the reduction can come from any part of the student's need-based financial aid package: Grants, subsidized loans, or work-study, depending on college policy and the student's circumstances, leaving many families waiting until the last minute to learn how much they'll need to pay.

Student loans are likewise disbursed directly to the college. The student only receives loan proceeds if there is money remaining after all direct costs are covered—tuition, fees, and on-campus room and board as applicable—and it can take a couple of weeks to get the remaining balance. For example, let's say a student lives off campus and takes out a loan for $10,000 to cover tuition, rent and food. The student's tuition, net of scholarships, is $6,000. That $10,000 is sent to the school. The college keeps $6,000 of the loan to cover the tuition and sends the remaining $4,000 to the student, which can then be used to pay rent and buy food.

It's a good idea to review your financial aid package *before* tuition payments are due. If your package includes federal loans (Direct Student Loans or parent PLUS loans) you won't actually see that money, because the amounts will be automatically subtracted from your balance due. Many parents are surprised to learn that they took out PLUS loans because the loan money went directly to the college and they never received it.

Colleges offer payment plans; however, they often come with a fee. You'll want to check the details before making a decision on payment plans. Alex's college charged a fee for payment plans for tuition, but allowed each semester's on-campus room and board to be divided into three monthly payments with no additional charge. In many cases, paying a fee for a payment plan can be the difference between covering costs out of pocket and taking out a loan, so a reasonable fee—say, less than the interest on a loan—for a payment plan can be a good choice. Just remember that an extra $100 per quarter for a payment plan will be $1,200 over four years.

On the subject of room and board, students who have a choice of meal plans will typically need to choose one prior to the start of the year. You are usually best off choosing less than you think your student might need, because schools generally allow students to upgrade their meal plan later but not to downgrade it. Your college's Facebook parents' page will have lots of guidance on which to choose. Policies vary about rolling over unused funds. Like dorm deposit refund policies, many of these rollover policies have become less generous post-pandemic.

When there's a choice of meal plans, one of the choices is often not to have one and to simply pay as you go. These can quickly get expensive for a lot of reasons; one of them is that many states exempt meal plans from sales tax but not a la carte meals.

## Why you shouldn't wait to borrow

According to Sallie Mae's 'How America Pays for College,' the average family covers college costs using a combination of savings, spending from income, student loans, scholarships, and gifts from others.[1] One curious item in the report: Just about every year, it shows that less than half of students borrow for college. And yet two-thirds of students graduate from college with student loan debt. Similarly curious: The 2021 report shows that the average amount borrowed by a student was $8,775—despite the federal Direct Student Loan limit of $7,500.

This points to a common mistake families make when paying for college: They spend down their savings until it's gone, and then cast about to make ends meet for the remainder. The end result is usually spending more money because some of the best, and least expensive, tools to pay for college have annual limits and need to be used every year to maximize the benefits.

A second problem with spending-our-savings-then-figuring-out-the-rest is it usually means a family isn't making college choices based on dollars available to pay for college. Hopefully, since you're reading this, that won't be you.

The most beneficial college spending plan uses each available source each year. That means using some savings, some spending from income (the parents' and the student's), some borrowing, and some tax credit every year. You created a budget that divided your savings by four not just for an exercise in elementary school math, but because that's usually the best way to use your savings.

If you spend all of your savings first, you might miss out on free money from tax credits, since the AOTC requires that you spend $4,000 from something other than a qualified savings account like a 529. In addition, like the students in 'How America Pays for College,' your borrowing needs in future years might exceed the Direct Student Loan amount, meaning you'll be taking on higher-cost debt like Parent PLUS loans or private student loans. Given the difference in interest rates between the Direct Student Loan and Parent PLUS Loan, it is cheaper to take out the maximum Direct Student Loan starting in the student's first year of college than to wait to borrow and then take out larger amounts in Parent PLUS loans.

## Gifts and family money

What about other people's savings? How do you layer that into your spending plan? In the old days—pre-FAFSA Simplification—it was important to wait until January 1 of the student's sophomore year of college to withdraw funds from a non-parent-owned 529. However, the FAFSA no longer asks about money paid on your behalf. While there would be no penalty for withdrawing from those accounts sooner, it still makes more sense to hold off on using those funds if you're eligible for need-based aid. By spending down the parents' accounts first, you reduce the assets that you need to report on the FAFSA.

One exception to this rule would be an instance where the grandparents have diminishing capacity, which is unfortunately common at that stage of life. If you are concerned about your parents' ability to manage your student's 529, then it's probably worth spending those dollars sooner even if it results in slightly less financial aid. Pro tip: Regardless of your parents' or relatives' cognitive states, if they are saving for your child's education, you should confirm that you are named as the "successor owner" on that 529 or other savings account. That way, if anything happens, your focus doesn't need to be on how to access your student's 529.

## Who gets the 529 distribution

You've spent years putting money into your 529; now it's time to take it out. Sounds easy, right? But you have choices. Your 529 distribution can go to the account owner (usually the parent), the account beneficiary (the student) or directly to the school. You may be saying, "There's no way in !@#$% I'm sending tens of thousands of dollars to my teenager!" but in fact that's often the best way to do it, so hear me out.

First, your tax filing is much easier if the student receives the distribution. Every college student receives a 1098-T Tuition Statement form from their college. The 1098-T shows tuition, fees, and course material costs paid directly to the school. It also shows scholarships that were paid directly to the school on the student's behalf, including institutional, federal, and outside scholarship or grant money. The 1098-T has the student's Social Security number on it.

Any year in which a distribution is made from a 529 plan, the plan sends a 1099-Q to the recipient of the distribution. If the distribution goes to the student, then the 1099-Q and the 1098-T will have the same Social Security number. If it goes to the parent, the 1098-T will have the parent's Social Security number. While you do not need to report a 1099-Q on your taxes unless you make a nonqualified distribution on which taxes are due, you are likely to get an IRS deficiency letter if a 1099-Q is issued for a Social Security number that didn't get a 1098-T. It's not a big deal to correct this, but if you're like most people, you probably don't want to interact with the IRS any more than necessary.

Second, if you make a nonqualified distribution, taxes are due on it. The taxes are assessed to the person who received the distribution and thus taxed at their rate. Your student is likely to be in a lower tax bracket than you, so the taxes will be less.

The other option is to have 529 distributions sent directly to the college. While this avoids both of the issues above, it isn't the best idea if you either receive need-based financial aid or claim the AOTC. Colleges are known to confuse 529 distributions with outside scholarships— picture the bursar's office in the weeks before school starts as checks pour in from thousands or tens of thousands of sources—and reduce the student's aid package. It's then up to the student to correct that and get their financial aid readjusted.

For tax credits, remember that tax credits can only be claimed for tuition and fees, not room and board. If you send your 529 funds to the college for tuition and fees and then pay out of pocket for room and board, you cannot claim the AOTC.

Students who live off campus should check their college's off-campus room and board allowance. Using 529 withdrawals for off-campus living expenses are qualified—meaning they're not subject to tax or penalty—as long as the withdrawal does not exceed the actual costs or the school's off-campus room and board allowance, whichever is less.

In my family, we set up an online savings account for each kid, then linked the online savings account to our checking account. We have 529 distributions sent to the kids' online savings accounts, then transfer them to our account and pay college bills via ACH from our account.

You can also withdraw from your 529 at any point during a year when you have college costs; you do not need to time your withdrawals with payment due dates. Your 1099-Q will only show the total amount withdrawn, not dates when funds were withdrawn.

And if your state offers a tax benefit for 529 contributions, you can continue to contribute and take the tax benefits while your student is in college, even if you're withdrawing from the account too. Just watch out for the tax benefit rules, especially in the final year. Many plans require that you have the deductible amount in the account on the last day of the year in order to claim the tax benefit. For example, if your state gives a tax deduction for $5,000 in contributions annually, you probably need to still have $5,000 in your account on December 31—meaning your final contribution should be the calendar year before your final payment.

On the subject of 529s, how do you withdraw any excess? If you're one of those fortunate families who ends up with more savings than you need, and no other student to spend it on, it's beneficial to plan your excess withdrawal strategy. It's likely that your student will be in the 0–10% federal tax bracket for the duration of their college career, so withdrawing a portion every year will keep tax costs to a minimum.

And remember, tax and penalty only apply to the earnings in the account, and no penalty is due if the account is overfunded due to scholarships.

## Using the American Opportunity Tax Credit

If you are eligible for the AOTC, your spending plan should include $4,000 annually from a non-529 source. This can include a student loan.

When factoring the AOTC into your budget, remember that since it's a tax credit, it gets paid to you through your tax bill: Either you reduce withholding or estimated payments and take home a larger portion of your paycheck each month, or you get a larger refund when you file your taxes. So make sure you're accounting for it however you receive it, because it's not going into a specific "college" bucket. But at $10,000 over four years, it's too big an amount to overlook.

Keep in mind the key elements in claiming the AOTC, too:

- You can claim it in four tax years, but your student will be in college during five tax years.

- The income threshold—AGI of $160,000 for married filers and $80,000 for head of household filers—is not indexed for inflation. If you are near that level, you'll probably want to claim the AOTC starting the first year you're eligible in case you end up not being eligible in later college years. The AOTC has a phaseout range up to $180,000 for married filers and $90,000 for head of household; above those thresholds, you get nothing.

- Qualified Higher Education Expenses for the AOTC are more limited than for 529s: tuition, fees, books, and required supplies. You cannot claim the AOTC for room and board expenses.

- You need to spend the AOTC-eligible money in the calendar year in which you claim the credit. If your college is on the quarter system, you'll make three tuition payments each year, with two payments made before December 31 of your student's first year of college and only one in the final calendar year of college. If they're on the semester system, you'll have two tuition payments each year and probably only make one tuition payment in the first calendar year of college. Depending on your scholarships, you might need to plan your AOTC claims around the years when you have enough tuition costs—and plan your book purchases, too.

- You have to claim the student on your tax return in order to claim the AOTC. This comes into play more often for divorced parents who alternate claiming the student on their taxes. If one parent is eligible for the AOTC and the other isn't, it's best for the eligible parent to claim the student. With parents getting a $500 tax credit, not a deduction or exemption, for students on their tax return, the dollar benefit of claiming the student is the same for either parent, but forgoing the AOTC is giving away $2,500 in free money in order to get $500. Not a great swap.

Eligibility for the AOTC is based on AGI. Your AGI is your total income—salary, dividend and interest income, capital gains, taxable distributions from retirement savings, business income, taxable Social Security benefits—minus a few items: Student loan interest, educator expenses, some alimony payments, as well as HSA and pre-tax retirement contributions.

Your AGI is on line 11 of your tax return. Go look it up if you're unsure whether you're eligible for the AOTC.

If you are close to eligibility, look at your overall picture, because you might be able to *get* eligible. If your AGI is a few thousand dollars over the limit and you're not maxing out retirement, you can increase your retirement contributions to get under the threshold. If it's a stretch to do that every year during college, look for the most beneficial years. The AOTC is per student, so it's worth $5,000 a year when you have two college students or $7,500 if you have three.

Remember that the $4,000 in expenses is also per student and should factor into your planning as well. It can make sense to use student loans to cover some or all of the $4,000. A Direct Student Loan for a first-year student at 4% interest would accrue $220 in interest each year, for a total of $880 over four years—far less than the tax credit.

## The math on multiple kids in college

The most beneficial spending plan also considers the family's entire college path. This might include years with one college student and years with multiple college students, so you might need to make some adjustments to that budget you've created.

For example, if you can pay $6,000 each year and you have two students who are two years apart, your contribution to their education will look something like this:

Year 1: $6,000 to older

Year 2: $6,000 to older

Year 3: $3,000 each to older and younger

Year 4: $3,000 each to older and younger

Year 5: $6,000 to younger

Year 6: $6,000 to younger

That might leave you relying more heavily on savings and other resources during the two years with multiple students. You might get a boost in financial aid in those years; despite changes to the FAFSA formula, the CSS Profile continues to account for multiple students in college and many colleges will continue considering siblings for institutional aid. But you might just need to cover that gap yourself.

You might also consider borrowing during the years of overlap. Again, consider the amount you can spend every year and how many years post-college you'd be okay with paying off student loans. Our example family might borrow $6,000 each year during the overlapping years and plan to repay those loans in the two years following the youngest student's graduation, essentially creating an eight-year college payment plan.

## To borrow, or not to borrow

The decision whether or not to borrow is one you can make at any point along the way, as long as you fill out the FAFSA. Many students know going into things that they'll be taking out the maximum Direct Student Loan every year. Other families use it some years and not others. Your budget will give you a sense of where borrowing fits for you. You might find you need to borrow in years with multiple college students, or in years with additional expenses such as study abroad.

If you are considering borrowing beyond the Direct Student Loan limit, you'll be best off if you think of the loans from the perspective of your spending plan. Which is to say, whatever amount you can afford annually for college is the amount you can afford annually for a few years after college to get those loans paid off. Unless you're in one of the special circumstances in Chapter 8 (student loans), you'll want to make sure that any money you borrow can be paid off quickly— and well before your retirement.

My husband and I have variable incomes, so we took the approach of "pay as much as you can out of pocket first." On the short list of pandemic silver linings is that Alex and Gabi's freshman year ended up costing quite a bit less than we had budgeted. With students being sent home in March of 2020, we saved one-quarter of room and board at one college and got a partial refund of costs we had paid and a rollover of unspent meal plan dollars at the other. We had not intended for the kids to borrow, but with no interest accruing on student loans in the 2020–2021 school year, we had each take the "interest free" loan for cash flow purposes. The end result of that was one student's 529 has exactly the right amount of money in it to pay for college. We continue contributing to the other 529 for both the state tax benefit and the tax-free growth in the account.

Gabi lives on campus so her bills are all paid directly to the college. She has every kind of scholarship: merit, financial aid, and an outside scholarship. I usually find out a couple of days ahead of the due date how much we actually need to pay. One year, her outside scholarship had the effect of reducing her grant; another year it eliminated her work-study; the third year the check arrived late and wasn't applied to her fall bill at all. That means I guesstimate how much to take out of her 529 prior to fall quarter's bill. Since we pay some out of pocket and some from her 529 each quarter, I don't worry about over-withdrawing. (If you do over-withdraw, you need to return the funds within 60 days or you'll be liable for taxes and penalties on the earnings for the nonqualified portion of the distribution.)

Alex lives in an apartment, so his tuition gets paid to the school and he gets a monthly draw from his 529 for rent and food. His scholarship is a fixed dollar amount, so even though it doesn't show up on the initial statement from the college, I can figure out what needs to be paid.

Your spending plan has a lot of pieces. Turn the page for a worksheet where you'll put them all together.

# WORKSHEET 14: SPENDING PLAN

To download this worksheet, go to howtopayforcollege.com/htpfc-book-worksheets.

Which college do you want to review?

_____

"Estimated Net Price" from the last tab?

_____

Assume tuition prices rise by how much each year?

_____

|  | Freshman Year | Sophomore Year | Junior Year | Senior Year | 4-Year Total |
|---|---|---|---|---|---|
| **Qualified Expenses** | | | | | |
| Qualified Education Expenses | $ | $ | $ | $ | $ |
| Covered by Savings/Outside Scholarships | $ | $ | $ | $ | $ |
| **Remaining Qualified Expenses** | | | | | |
|  | $ | $ | $ | $ | $ |
| **Nonqualified Expenses** | | | | | |
| Clothing & Personal | $ | $ | $ | $ | $ |
| Insurance | $ | $ | $ | $ | $ |
| Transportation | $ | $ | $ | $ | $ |
| **Total Nonqualified Expenses** | | | | | |
|  | $ | $ | $ | $ | $ |
| **Total Remaining Expenses** | | | | | |
|  | $ | $ | $ | $ | $ |

## Income Available

| Annual Income from Parents | $ | $ | $ | $ | $ |
|---|---|---|---|---|---|
| Annual Income from Student | $ | $ | $ | $ | $ |
| Annual Income from Others | $ | $ | $ | $ | $ |
| American Opportunity Tax Credit | $ | $ | $ | $ | $ |
| Work-Study | $ | $ | $ | $ | $ |
| Other | $ | $ | $ | $ | $ |
| **Total Income Available** | | | | | |
| | $ | $ | $ | $ | |
| **Total Surplus/ Need** | $ | $ | $ | $ | $ |
| **Direct Student Loan** | $ | $ | $ | $ | $ |
| **Additional Borrowing Need** | $ | $ | $ | $ | $ |
| **Total Debt** | $ | $ | $ | $ | $ |

## Notes

_____

_____

_____

_____

# TO-DO LIST

KNOWLEDGE IS POWER, as the saying goes, but it's only powerful if you use it. So before you close this book and move on to the next thing, let's build a to-do list so that what you've learned becomes a superpower. And if you haven't yet downloaded the worksheets, go to howtopayforcollege.com/htpfc-book-worksheets right now and do it. Updating the worksheets as your college search progresses will help keep your compass pointed in the right direction as you go through the college search journey.

- Remind yourself again, *Why College?* Personal growth. Education. New people. New experiences. Review and update your worksheets from Chapter 1 and Chapter 2 to reinforce your values and priorities.

- Talk to your student. Talk about why you want them going to college, and talk to them about what college costs, how you intend to support them, and what commitment they need to have. Review the Chapter 3 worksheet for conversation prompts around goals and money.

- Set up or ramp up your savings. More savings will give you more choices. Chapter 5's worksheet will get you started and help you do more.

- Understand your budget. You will find good choices that fit your budget, as long as you use your budget to guide your choices. Chapter 10's budget worksheet is your friend here, and downloading it will make it an even better friend, one that you can update.

- Review how the FAFSA works and implement strategies to improve your chances of receiving financial aid while you still have time. Chapter 4's worksheet outlines steps you can take to maximize aid eligibility via the FAFSA and CSS Profile—and if you use the downloadable version you can calculate the approximate impact of those strategies.

- Look at how best to position your student for merit scholarships, and look for outside scholarships that can help fill the cost gap. Complete Chapter 6's merit aid profile to identify and pursue scholarship opportunities.

- Review the options to stretch your budget, including student loans. The worksheets for Chapters 8 and 9 will help you to understand borrowing and find other options to bring costs in line with your budget.

- Do your homework. You've got a set of research tools so you and your student can find lots of good choices. The worksheets for Chapters 11 and 12 will help you to both cast a wide net and narrow your list down to a good set of choices.

- Set up your spending plan and stick with it. The final two worksheets, for Chapters 13 and 14, will help you make sure that your college choice fits your family's financial situation.

# CONCLUSION

WHEN MY KIDS left for college, I wrote each of them a sappy letter, wrapped it up with a framed favorite photo of them, and left it in their college dresser drawer. Each letter was about how the lessons they had learned growing up would help them become their future self.

For Alex, I included a picture of him and his sister after a soccer game where he had scored the winning goal. He worked so hard that year at soccer, both at training and on his own, and we loved seeing the success that his efforts had brought. Gabi was carrying his water bottle, which to me was a perfect encapsulation of so many lessons: putting in the effort and seeing the results, and having the support of those who love you while you're on your journey.

Gabi's picture was of a solo she performed in a school musical, with her standing surrounded by her friends in the theater program. A similar set of lessons: work hard, see the results, and value the people on the journey with you.

Now that we've spent all this time together, I feel like I want to impart to you some similar commencement wisdom and sappy encouragement. Planning for your child's college is the ultimate balancing act of parenting. You want their future to be unlimited, and it's painful to impose limits on it no matter how important it is to do so. You know how hard they've worked, and you want that effort to be acknowledged in the form of college acceptances.

When your student selects their college, they are standing in the gateway between their past and their future: A Rubicon of sorts in their coming of age journey. For years, so much behavior has been motivated by "so you can go to a good college." So many choices have been made on the basis of "so you can go to a good college." And now they're waiting to be accepted to those good colleges, or weighing their acceptance decision, or even packing their bags.

Here's what you need to know now: Wherever you are in this process, you have good choices available to you. With this book as your guide, you have the tools and knowledge to make good decisions.

I want to reassure you when this feels stressful that your student has a bright future. And guess what? Their future is bright because of who they are. Going to college will help them become a more educated, knowledgeable version of themselves, one who's more prepared to go out into the world on their own. But that self is what makes them special now and what will make them successful in the future.

Like so many things in life, if you put in the effort, you'll get the results. Same goes with college. You've got this. And so does your kid.

# GLOSSARY

**1098-T:** A tax form issued by colleges showing tuition and fees paid and scholarships received.

**529:** A college savings account allowing tax-free growth and distributions. Most 529s are run by states, many of which offer tax benefits to residents for their contributions. Others are run by private entities. Savings in 529s can be used at any college that participates in the federal student aid system.

**529 Savings Plan:** The most common form of 529, where participants choose an investment portfolio and their savings grow based on investment performance.

**Adjusted gross income (AGI):** The amount on line 11 of your federal tax return. Essentially this is your total income less contributions to retirement and a few other adjustments.

**Aid packaging:** The process by which a financial aid office creates a student's financial aid package. The package can include grants, loans and work-study. It may or may not meet a student's demonstrated need.

**Annuity:** An insurance-based investment that is commonly sold to parents who are told that it doesn't count as an asset on the FAFSA. While that's true, it does count on the CSS Profile, and these products generally have very high costs associated with them. One of those costs is a commission, meaning the big winner when you buy an annuity is the person who sold it to you.

**AOTC:** The American Opportunity Tax Credit is a $2,500 per year tax credit available for four years of undergraduate education.

**Asset protection allowance:** The amount of assets parents are allowed to have but not report on the FAFSA.

**Cash flow:** The money you have available from your income after you've paid all of your expenses such as mortgage or rent, utilities, groceries, etc.

**College vs university:** With apologies to those outside the U.S., these terms are used interchangeably throughout this book.

**Common App:** A college application platform allowing students to apply to multiple colleges via a single application. Most U.S. colleges and many international colleges accept the Common App.

**Community college:** Two-year, state-run colleges offering associate's degrees and other certifications.

**Cost of attendance:** The published price of a college, including tuition, fees, room, board, books, supplies and personal expenses.

**CPI-W:** One version of the Consumer Price Index which is used in the FAFSA formula. (There are multiple versions of CPI.)

**CSS Profile:** An additional financial aid form used by many private colleges to calculate student financial need.

**Decision Day:** May 1 is the date by which virtually all colleges require an enrollment response from all students (other than those who applied early decision).

**Demonstrated need (financial need):** The difference between a student's EFC or SAI (as calculated by the FAFSA and/or CSS Profile) and a college's Cost of Attendance.

**Direct Student Loan:** Federal student loans available for the undergraduate years. These have the lowest interest rates and fees of any federal education loan but also the lowest annual limits

($5,500 for first-year students, $6,500 for second year, and $7,500 for subsequent years.).

**Early Action (EA):** An admissions option where a student applies early to one or more colleges, receives an acceptance (or decline) early, but has until May 1 to decide whether or not to enroll.

**Early Decision (ED):** An admissions option where a student applies early to their first-choice college and, if accepted, must enroll.

**Education loan:** Money borrowed by the student or parent to pay for college. I use this term primarily when talking about loans taken out by parents.

**Expected family contribution (EFC):** The amount the FAFSA and CSS Profile calculate as the family's ability to contribute financially to college each year. This has been renamed the Student Aid Index or SAI.

**FAFSA:** The Free Application for Federal Student Aid. This is a form required by all colleges in order for a student to be considered for financial aid on the basis of need. It's also the application for federal student loans.

**Financial aid:** Scholarships, grants, loans and work-study offered to close the gap between a college's cost of attendance and a student's Demonstrated Need.

**For-profit college:** Colleges that operate for the purpose of maximizing revenue. Many of these offer two-year or certificate programs rather than bachelor's degree programs.

**Grant:** Scholarship money awarded on the basis of financial need.

**Independent students:** Students who provide their own financial support. The FAFSA has a very strict definition of independent student; it's not just one who files their own tax return.

**Institutional merit scholarship:** A merit scholarship offered by the college.

**Merit scholarship:** A scholarship awarded on the basis of the student's abilities, whether academic, athletic or anything else.

**Net cost/Net price:** The annual cost you would pay to attend a college once financial aid and scholarships have been subtracted from published Cost of Attendance.

**Net price calculator:** A tool each college is required to offer that allows a student to input their data (financial and sometimes academic) and see what students like them received in scholarships and grants in the previous school year.

**Non-education loan:** Any form of borrowing that families use other than a student loan, such as a home equity line of credit. A key differentiator between student loans—federal and private—and non-education loans is that student loans do not require payments to be made during the college years.

**Nonqualified distribution:** A withdrawal from a 529 for an ineligible expense. These distributions are subject to income tax (federal and state) and a 10% penalty on the earnings portion of the withdrawal.

**Outside scholarship:** A scholarship awarded by any entity other than the college.

**Parent PLUS Loan:** Federal education loans available to parents. These have higher interest rates and fees than Direct Student Loans, but parents can borrow up to the full cost of attendance net of financial aid and scholarships.

**Prepaid Tuition Plan:** A form of 529 where you buy tuition credits at current rates; these credits are redeemed in the future at either their then-current value or some other multiple. These can only be used for tuition expenses, not room and board or books.

**Private college/university/school:** In this book, "private ___" refers to private nonprofit institutions. These are what we traditionally think of when thinking of private schools—four-year-degree-granting institutions that offer scholarships and other forms of financial aid. Nonprofit colleges are required to invest any surplus in the school.

**Private loan:** Any student loan offered by a private lender such as a bank.

**Public college:** A college or university that receives its funding primarily from a state or other governmental jurisdiction. Typically public colleges give preference to students who live within that jurisdiction.

**QHEE:** Qualified Higher Education Expense. An expense for which you can use your 529 or claim the AOTC; as noted elsewhere in the book, 529s and the AOTC each have different definitions of QHEE. For example, room and board are QHEEs for 529 money but not for the AOTC.

**Regional Tuition Exchange:** A consortium of public colleges in a geographic region that offers tuition discounts to students within that region.

**Student Aid Index (SAI):** The amount the FAFSA and CSS Profile calculate as the family's ability to contribute financially to college each year. Formerly called the EFC.

**Scholarship:** Scholarship money awarded on any basis other than financial need.

**Scholarship renewal:** The requirements to continue receiving a scholarship beyond the first year in which it's awarded.

**Self-help aid:** Any part of a student's financial aid package that is not a grant or scholarship. Generally this is work-study or loans.

**Student Aid Estimator:** A tool that estimates a student's EFC or SAI. Previously called the FAFSA4caster. It's available at studentaid.gov.

**Student loan:** Money borrowed by the student to pay for college. Student loans can be taken from the federal government via the FAFSA or from private lenders.

**Subsidized loans:** A federal Direct Student Loan on which no interest accrues while the student is in college and during the six-month grace period following graduation. These are awarded on the basis of financial need.

**Work-study:** Student employment that is awarded as part of a financial aid package.

# ACKNOWLEDGMENTS

When I started this book project I thought that writing was a solitary pursuit. Along the way I've learned that it's truly a team sport, and I'm extraordinarily grateful to the entire team who saw me through this. My high school English teacher always said, "To list is to omit" so let me start with a huge thank you to everyone—family, friends, colleagues, blog readers, friendly strangers and more—whose support and encouragement made this possible. A special few made it not just possible but *done*:

Alex and Gabi, thank you for letting me record and share this part of your lives. Not every parent gets a chance to brag about their kids to this degree! It's my privilege to be part of your journey, and I am so excited to see where life takes you next—or more likely, where you take it. I promise not to write any more books about you.

Bob, thanks for the extra dishes, cooking, housework, website design, reading drafts, finding other things to do on the weekend when I needed quiet, encouragement, ego stroking and so much more. All of this is better because you're a part of it.

Huge thanks to Carl Richards who took the blindfold off so that I could run this obstacle course. I can honestly say that without your encouragement and assistance this book would not exist.

I can't say enough good things about my book ladies, Andrea Vedder, Sarah Wexler and Beth Kempton. You turned my chaos into clarity and gave me the tools and confidence to become an author.

Craig Pearce, Chris Parker, Nick Fletcher and the team at Harriman House: Somehow you all know exactly what to say to keep me on track through a long and daunting process. Thank you for your encouragement and polite nudges in the right direction.

My team at Independent Progressive Advisors, Scott Emblen and Becky Meats, has been relentless in picking up slack and giving me the flexibility to actually do this. I'll thank you by returning the favor!

# ENDNOTES

## Chapter 1

1 Bureau of Labor Statistics, 'Monthly Labor Review.' Available at bls.gov/opub/mlr/2013/article/pdf/marriage-and-divorce-patterns-by-gender-race-and-educational-attainment.pdf.

2 Social Security Administration Office of Retirement Policy Research Summary November 2015.

3 Bureau of Labor Statistics.

4 Federal Reserve Board, 'Consumer & Community Context.' January 2019. Available at www.valuepenguin.com/news/student-loan-debt-home-ownership-link.

5 Economics of Education Review Volume 53, August 2016, Pages 207–216. Available at www.sciencedirect.com/science/article/abs/pii/S0272775716302035.

6 National Bureau of Economic Research: 'Estimating the Payoff to Attending a More Selective College: An Application of Selection on Observables and Unobservables.' Available at www.nber.org/papers/w7322.

## Chapter 2

1 Federal Reserve Bank of New York: 'Credit Supply and the

Rise in College Tuition.' Available at academic.oup.com/rfs/article/32/2/423/5042299.

2    National Center for Education Statistics. Available at nces.ed.gov/programs/digest/d19/tables/dt19_303.70.asp.

## Chapter 4

1    Lyndon B Johnson Presidential Library.

2    Bureau of Labor Statistics, 'Monthly Labor Review.' Available at bls.gov/opub/mlr/2013/article/pdf/marriage-and-divorce-patterns-by-gender-race-and-educational-attainment.pdf.

## Chapter 5

1    Sallie Mae, 'How America Pays for College.' Available at www.salliemae.com/content/dam/slm/writtencontent/Research/HowAmericaPaysforCollege2021.pdf.

## Chapter 9

1    IRS, www.irs.gov/credits-deductions/individuals/llc.

2    'National Association of Colleges and Employers 2021 Internship & Co-op Survey Report.' Available at career.fsu.edu/sites/g/files/upcbnu746/files/2021-nace-internship-and-co-op-survey-executive-summary.pdf.

## Chapter 14

1    Sallie Mae, 'How America Pays for College.' Available at www.salliemae.com/content/dam/slm/writtencontent/Research/HowAmericaPaysforCollege2021.pdf.

# INDEX

# ABOUT THE AUTHOR

Ann Garcia, CFP®, has helped thousands of families—including her own—save millions of dollars on college. Ann is the managing partner of Independent Progressive Advisors, a fee-only financial advisor, and the author of The College Financial Lady blog. Ann and her husband, Bob, live in Portland, OR. Their twins are away from home attending (affordable) colleges.

CPSIA information can be obtained
at www.ICGtesting.com
Printed in the USA
BVHW052214070523
663698BV00009B/6